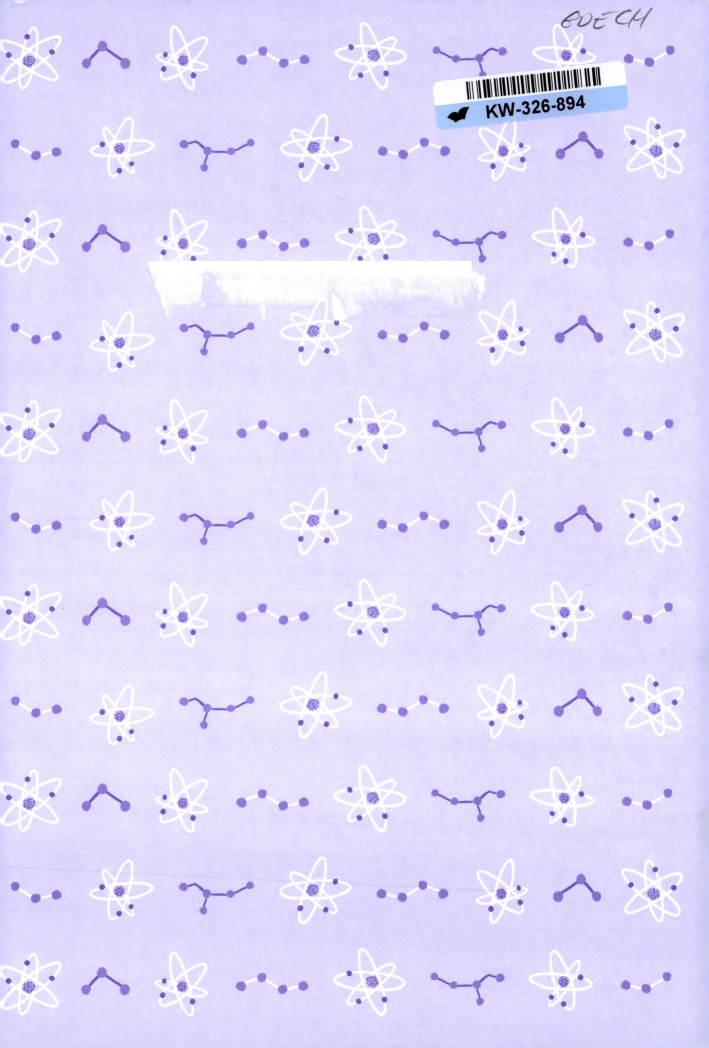

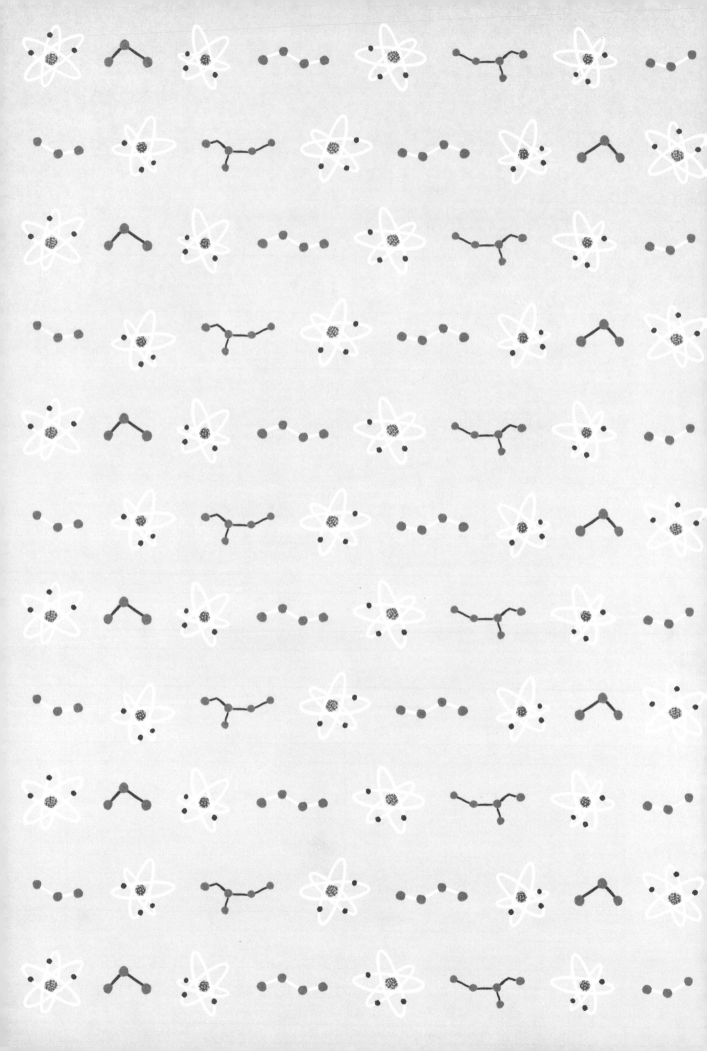

THE BEDTIME BOOK OF IMPOSSIBLE QUESTIONS

For everyone who doesn't take
'I don't know' for an answer – I.T.

To Fionn, if ever I don't know an
answer, please refer to this – A.C.

BLOOMSBURY CHILDREN'S BOOKS
Bloomsbury Publishing Plc
50 Bedford Square, London, WC1B 3DP, UK
29 Earlsfort Terrace, Dublin 2, Ireland

BLOOMSBURY, BLOOMSBURY CHILDREN'S BOOKS and the Diana logo
are trademarks of Bloomsbury Publishing Plc

First published in Great Britain 2022 by Bloomsbury Publishing Plc

A catalogue record for this book is available from the British Library

ISBN: HB: 978-1-5266-2375-1; eBook: 978-1-5266-2753-7
2 4 6 8 10 9 7 5 3

Printed and bound in the UK by Bell & Bain Ltd.

To find out more about our authors and books visit www.bloomsbury.com and sign up for our newsletters

THE BEDTIME BOOK OF IMPOSSIBLE QUESTIONS

Real life adventures in curiosity

Isabel Thomas

illustrated by
Aaron Cushley

BLOOMSBURY
CHILDREN'S BOOKS

LONDON   OXFORD   NEW YORK   NEW DELHI   SYDNEY

Contents

Shall I tell you a secret?

Science isn't about knowing lots of facts or getting the right answer all the time. It's not even about wearing a lab coat.

Science is about **asking questions**.

They can be sensible questions.

They can be silly questions.

Best of all, they can be

IMPOSSIBLE QUESTIONS!

How do chickens lay eggs?

What came first, chickens or eggs?

If chickens are so delicious, why don't they eat themselves?

The history of science is paved with **impossible questions**.

Each one is a stepping stone on the path to understanding the universe and everything in it.

But this path is not yet finished …

Every answer leads to **new** impossible questions … and new stepping stones!

This book explores some of the impossible questions that are still **bamboozling** biologists, confusing chemists and making physicists feel **perplexed**.

None of the answers are 100 per cent correct – as any scientist will tell you, there is **no such thing as a perfect answer**!

They are just our best answers based on the **evidence** available right now. As scientists continue to **experiment**, **explore**, **collect** and **discover** more information, the answers will probably change.

The impossible questions in this book will help you explore life, the universe and everything in it – and the best time to do this (as every scientist knows) is at bedtime.

Talk about the answers, share your ideas, and come up with your own impossible questions.

Impossible Questions Chart

Impossible
Perplexed
Confused
Bamboozled

7.00pm   7.15pm   7.30pm   Lights Out Time

Why does rain smell rainy?

Next time it rains, go outside and take a **big sniff**. After dry days, a rain shower can make the air smell clean, sweet, fresh and earthy – rather like a walk in the woods. Lots of people like this smell and it even has a name – petrichor (say peh-truh-kaw). It's not the smell of raindrops themselves, because pure water doesn't have a smell. It actually comes from microbes that live in the soil. Every teaspoon of soil contains **up to a billion** of these tiny living things. They do a very important job – feeding on dead leaves and other things that were once alive, recycling the minerals that new life needs to grow. As they go about their lives, microbes make an oil called geosmin. When **raindrops splatter** on dusty, dry soil, tiny particles of geosmin are thrown up into the air and get carried away on the wind ... **eventually reaching our noses!** Nobody knows exactly why the microbes make geosmin. One idea is that they might be trying to hitch a lift to new homes on the animals and insects that come to snuffle the lovely smell. If you like the smell, you don't have to wait for a rainy day – beetroot plants make geosmin too!

So you could say that beetroot tastes like a rainy day!

Could I touch a rainbow?

Sadly, a rainbow is not a solid object that we can touch. It's more like millions of moving mirrors made of water. You see a rainbow when **sunlight bounces off raindrops** towards your eyes. For this to happen, you have to be standing with your back to the sun, looking towards a rainy part of the sky (or even water being sprayed by a hose!). Sunlight is a mixture of different colours. As sunlight travels into a raindrop, it slows down a little and changes direction. This splits the sunlight up into its different colours. The coloured light then **bounces off** the back of the raindrop, as if it were a mirror. If you happen to be looking that way, the light reaches your eyes. Each raindrop reflects a single colour towards your eyes, but when you look towards a rainy sky you are seeing **millions of drops at once**. Together, they reflect red, orange, yellow, green, blue, indigo and violet light towards your eyes. Your brain tries to make sense of this trick of the light. It tells you that you're looking at a flat, colourful circle somewhere in the distance. Up close, we can't see the colours reflected by raindrops. So you can't touch a rainbow that you can see. But you could go and stand in the rain that's making a rainbow for somebody else.

From the ground you only see part of the colourful circle, which is why most rainbows look like arches.

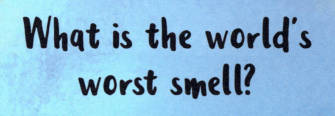

What is the world's worst smell?

Your nose can sniff out at least a trillion different smells, but it's your brain's job to tell you if they're nasty or nice. Everyone's brain is different, but there are some odours that most people agree are DISGUSTING. One of these is skatole, the substance that gives **poo** its smell. Although it's revolting in big doses, a little skatole can smell lovely and sweet – it gives flowers such as jasmine their scent and is even used to flavour vanilla ice cream! Another well-known pong is skunk spray, a smelly substance containing sulphur. Predators squirted by skunks **stink for up to three weeks**!

Chemicals that contain sulphur are to blame for lots of other awful smells too, including rotten **eggs, stinky socks and farts**. But believe it or not, there are even worse smells! When a metal called selenium combines with hydrogen, it makes a famously foul gas called hydrogen selenide. This is not something you would **ever** want to sniff – one whiff can wipe out a person's sense of smell for hours, and a big dose can be deadly. Scientists who have sniffed hydrogen selenide and survived have compared it to rotting radishes, or the smell of six skunks and a burning tyre! What's the worst whiff you have ever sniffed? How would you describe it to somebody else?

Why do we need two ears?

Have you ever listened to a bedtime story while lying on a pillow? Perhaps you're doing it right now. Even with one ear blocked or covered, we can still hear pretty well. So why do our bodies go to the trouble of growing two? Well, imagine you are Little Red Riding Hood, strolling through a **dark, dark forest**. Suddenly you hear a rustle and a growl. You can't see the wolf, but thanks to your two ears you can hear **exactly** where the sound is coming from – and **run in the other direction**! Because your ears are on opposite sides of your head, each one collects slightly different sounds. So if a twig snaps to your left, your left ear will hear the sound just before your right ear does, and a little more loudly. Your brain quickly compares the information from both ears to work out where the sound is coming from. Try it for yourself, by sitting with your eyes closed and pointing to the sounds you hear around you. But if you hear a wolf don't point – RUN!

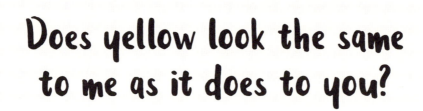

Does yellow look the same to me as it does to you?

We all agree that bananas are yellow, and oranges are orange. But what if the colour that I see when I look at a banana is actually the colour you see when you look at an orange, or a pear? **Are we really seeing the same thing**, or have we just learned to call different colours by the same name? It's impossible to know for certain, because we'll never be able to look through someone else's eyes. But we have found some clues that people do see colours differently.

The average person has eyes that can detect three different types of light – red, green and blue light. These colours can be combined in different ways to make millions of other colours. Most people's eyes can detect about a million different combinations, but it's our brains that make sense of this information to decide what colours we are seeing. And it turns out that it's pretty easy to trick your brain! One person can see the same colour very differently depending on which other colours are nearby, or even how he or she is feeling. This means that different people probably do see colours differently, but does it matter? No matter how we see a banana, **it still tastes just as good!**

These circles are all yellow. When they are criss-crossed by different coloured lines, our brains get confused and see them as different colours!

How long are millipedes?

It's easy to measure one millipede, but it's **impossible** to answer this question for millipedes in general. For starters, scientists think there may be **80,000** different kinds of millipedes! The tiniest are just over 3 mm long – a little shorter than a grain of rice, while the largest millipedes can grow longer than an adult's forearm! Even millipedes of the same species can be very different lengths, depending on how good they are at finding food, and how many birthdays they've had. Unlike humans, some millipedes **keep on growing** for their entire lives by **adding new segments** to their bodies. Each new segment has two pairs of legs – it's lucky they don't need school shoes. Long or short, millipedes are needed by forests around the world. They chomp away at dead leaves that gather on the forest floor, breaking them down so that all the nutrients trapped inside can be recycled and used by new living things. Although the word 'millipede' means 'thousand feet', no one has ever found a millipede with 1,000 legs. The record is around 750 legs, and strangely these belong to some of the shortest millipedes!

14

Why don't humans have tails?

Most animals with a backbone also have a tail that sticks out behind their body. Imagine what you could do if you had one too! You could **swish** it in water to help you swim, or **wag** it to say hello. It would help you **balance** as you run and jump, or **grasp** branches while you clamber up trees. You could use it by day to swat flies from your food and by night to keep your nose warm. Tails are very useful indeed – **so why don't we get one?** Humans do have tailbones at the very end of our spines. They are tiny and tucked away, but they tell us that our ancestors had tails. Great apes like chimpanzees, gorillas and gibbons have lost their tails too, so we can look at them to **find clues**. Being tailless seems to help these animals move around with straight backs, and their heads held high. Monkeys can't do this – **their tails get in the way!** It's impossible to know for sure why we lost our tails because we can't zoom back millions of years and watch it happen. Perhaps having smaller tails helped our ancestors to stand, walk and run more easily on two legs, saving energy which they could use for other things. Our tails became less useful, and eventually **disappeared**. Leaving our tails behind has been no problem. We can still swim, say hello, balance, climb, swat flies and keep warm – we just do it in different ways.

Could a tortoise really win a race with a hare?

The Tortoise and the Hare is one of the world's most famous stories. But could a slow, heavy tortoise really beat a speedy hare? Scientists love an impossible question, and one team took on this challenge. They discovered that slower, steadier animals really do move faster (and further) than speedy ones over the course of their lives! Animals that can move very quickly in short bursts, like hares, actually move less overall. They spend long periods of time resting and snoozing – just like the hare in the story. Meanwhile, slow tortoises plod around feeding all day, every day – racking up long-distance records. Which type of animal do you think we are?

15

How many words are there?

At least **7,000 different languages** are spoken around the world, and each language has thousands (or even hundreds of thousands) of words. It's impossible to count them all, but people who write dictionaries try their best. The Oxford English Dictionary is one of the chunkiest. It lists more than **170,000 words** in the English language. But English and other **languages are always changing** – people stop using some words and invent new ones. Anyone can invent a word, but it only becomes part of a language once it's used and understood by other people. An English writer from the 1600s called William Shakespeare was brilliant at introducing new words – 'bedroom', 'eyeball', 'hurry' and 'lonely' are just some of the 1,700 words that he made popular.

In ten years time we'll all be using words that don't exist right now. Perhaps you'll even invent some yourself!

What do we need a new word for? Try inventing one. You could change the meaning of an existing word or put two words together to make a brand new one.

Can I learn to speak to animals?

Once there was a gorilla called Koko, who became famous for 'speaking' a human language. She learned to understand **2,000 words** and could even make signs with her hands to say what she wanted and how she was feeling. Humans don't seem to be as good at learning to understand the sounds that animals make, but many scientists think **it's possible** if we try. Most of us only hear simple squeaks, chirps, barks or growls when we listen to animals.

However, scientists who have spent weeks or months with animals such as prairie dogs, bonobos and dolphins, have discovered that these animals use **lots of different sounds** to 'say' different things. One scientist even counted eleven different noises made by a group of guinea pigs! They whistle when hungry, thirsty or scared, *chut* when they are exploring, and *drrr* when they want to raise the alarm. We'll probably never be able to gossip with a guinea pig or chat with a chimpanzee, but one day we may be able to listen in on the secrets that animals tell each other.

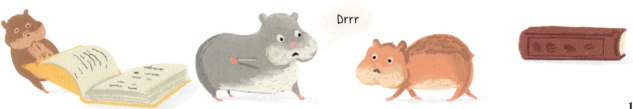

Drrr

How do we know that unicorns have never existed?

We can all describe a dinosaur or doodle a unicorn, even though we've never seen either in real life. But how do we know that dinosaurs once **stomped about the planet,** while unicorns **exist only in myths,** legends and our imaginations? It's impossible to travel back in time, but we can use fossils to work out which animals used to live on Earth. Fossils form when part of an animal – like a **bone or a footprint** – gets preserved in rock. If we find a fossil, we know that the creature that it came from must have once lived on our planet. We can even work out when that animal lived by measuring how old the rock is. Humans have found fossils from about 800 different types of dinosaurs, but no one has ever found a unicorn fossil. Until we do, our best theory is that unicorns are not real. **So, where do all the stories come from?** Why do unicorns pop up everywhere, from pyjamas to coins?

People have been telling unicorn stories for thousands of years. One of the first came from an ancient Greek book, which describes a huge, white horse with a **colourful horn** in the middle of its forehead. It wasn't a story book – **the author thought unicorns were completely real!** More than 1,000 years later, the famous Italian explorer Marco Polo also wrote about seeing real unicorns. In the days before cameras were invented, these tales would have been easy to believe. After all, a horse with a horn doesn't seem that strange compared to a **giant beast** with a nose that works like a hand (an elephant) or a green, **clawed reptile** that can swallow a person whole (a crocodile). And there really are animals with horns on their foreheads, such as narwhals and rhinos. Perhaps Marco and other adventurers had seen one of these, and just weren't very good at describing it. We still love to tell unicorn stories, but we don't have to go far to find real-life animals that are just as magical.

Could I swim in ice cream?

Imagine that the world's **biggest** ice cream has melted, leaving behind a puddle of strawberry, vanilla and chocolate gloop. It's thicker than water – and much more delicious! **But could you swim in it?** To find out, a team of scientists added buckets of guar gum to the water in a swimming pool. Guar gum is an ingredient that makes ice cream thicker. It made the liquid in the pool twice as **gloopy** as water.

Next, the scientists found some excellent swimmers and challenged them to dive in. Amazingly, the swimmers found they could paddle just as quickly as swimmers in a normal pool! Although it was harder to move their arms and legs, the gloopy liquid didn't move out of the way as easily as water does. With each push of their hands or feet, the ice cream mix pushed back much harder than water – sending them forwards with more force. This shows that you could swim in ice cream, if you melted it first. But **DON'T** try this at home – **it's much more fun to eat it!**

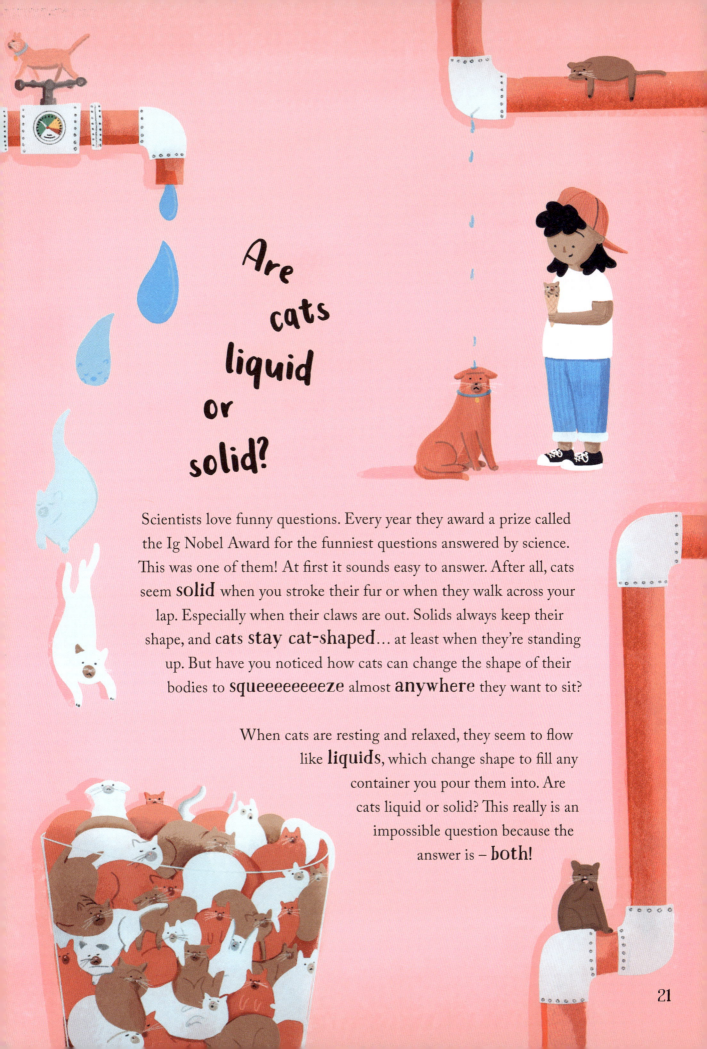

Are cats liquid or solid?

Scientists love funny questions. Every year they award a prize called the Ig Nobel Award for the funniest questions answered by science. This was one of them! At first it sounds easy to answer. After all, cats seem **solid** when you stroke their fur or when they walk across your lap. Especially when their claws are out. Solids always keep their shape, and **cats stay cat-shaped**… at least when they're standing up. But have you noticed how cats can change the shape of their bodies to **squeeeeeeeeze** almost **anywhere** they want to sit?

When cats are resting and relaxed, they seem to flow like **liquids,** which change shape to fill any container you pour them into. Are cats liquid or solid? This really is an impossible question because the answer is – **both!**

If you can feel bitter, do other feelings have tastes?

We have a big choice of words for talking about things that happen around us. Think of all the ways to describe what you see, smell, taste, hear and touch. It can be much harder to describe the feelings and emotions happening inside our bodies. Sometimes simple words like *sad*, *happy* and *angry* just aren't enough. That's why we can use our senses to help explain to other people EXACTLY how we are feeling. If someone says they are *bitterly disappointed*, we think of bitter foods and drinks that leave a sharp, unpleasant taste in our mouths – it's a good way to describe a nasty feeling that hangs around. We can use tastes to help us describe nice feelings too. You might hear people talk about the *sweet taste of success*, or *sweet relief*! When we say someone is being sweet, it means they are making us feel good. We can even feel *bittersweet* – a mixture of happy and sad at the same time. Like when you win a prize, but your best friend loses out. These tasty (or not-so-tasty) words fill our heads with pictures of familiar foods, which help us understand how someone else is feeling.

SOUR

So, are we just playing with words, or do different emotions actually cause us to taste different things? Several teams of scientists have tried to find out. One study found that sweet tastes activate the same parts of our brain as **happy emotions**, while bitter tastes activate the 'unhappy' parts of our brain. This is a clue that **tastes and emotions are actually linked**.

One team of scientists asked sports fans to taste two different ice creams after watching hockey matches (it might have been the most fun experiment EVER!). Although the two ice cream flavours were the same each time, the fans said they tasted **sweeter** after their team won a match, and **sourer** when their team lost a match! Another study found that, for some people, just thinking about love made water taste sweeter! It's good to share our emotions, so practice playing with words to tell people how you feel – there are no rules! Which tastes could you use to describe emotions like surprise or excitement? Which emotions might be described as sour or salty? And, for an extra challenge, can you describe any tastes using emotions?

How does gravity work?

Try throwing an object up into the air (not this book!). Something makes it change direction and travel back down to your hand, or to the ground. **We call this something** *gravity*. Every time you fall over, use a slide or try to leap off the planet into space, gravity brings you back down to Earth with a bump! It's easy to see gravity at work around us. Explaining how it works is much harder. That doesn't stop scientists from having a go.

Idea 1: About 330 years ago, an English scientist called Isaac Newton said that **we can think of gravity as an invisible force**. His idea was that every object, big or small, has a gravitational force that pulls other objects towards it. You are pulled towards the Earth … and the Earth is pulled towards you. There is even a tiny pull between you and this book! But Newton explained that bigger objects have more gravitational force than smaller ones, so we only notice the pull of massive objects like planets and moons. He also worked out that the closer we are to an object, the more we feel the pull of its gravitational force. Newton's invisible glue was a very useful idea. It explained why on Earth small things fall to the ground, but also why huge planets stay in orbit around the Sun (zoom to page 27 to find out how). It also explains why some objects are heavier than others – denser, heavier objects simply have more stuff packed inside them for Earth's gravitational force to pull on! Newton used his idea to write laws describing how things behave, and these laws have been really useful. They have even helped us work out how to beat gravity, and launch satellites, telescopes and people into space. But as people **explored more of the universe**, we began to notice all the things that Newton's idea couldn't explain – like a **strange wobble** in Mercury's orbit around the Sun, or how this 'invisible force' actually worked!

Idea 2: Just over 200 years later, the German physicist Albert Einstein came up with a completely different idea to explain how gravity works. He said that **gravity is not a force** at all! It's just a side effect that happens when massive objects 'bend' space. Before we can understand how this works, we need to think about space differently. Instead of a big, empty area of nothingness, think about it like a sheet of stretchy fabric. If you put a big, heavy ball on the sheet of stretchy fabric, it will be warped (bent out of shape). The same thing happens to the fabric of space – but in 3D. Every object in the universe – from tiny atoms, to massive stars – **bends this space fabric out of shape**. The more massive an object is, the more it bends the fabric of space! When space is bent, it changes how nearby objects move. A planet, spacecraft or even a ray of light travelling through space might appear to change its path when it gets near a massive planet or star, but it's really following the same path through space – the path itself has just been curved out of shape!

Imagine a meteorite zooming through space in a straight line. When it gets near Earth, its path seems to change. It crashes to the ground. Let's ask Newton and Einstein to explain why.

Both ideas are really useful for **predicting** how things will behave. They are also used to design everything from space rockets to navigation systems. But it's impossible to say that either of them absolutely, 100 per cent explains gravity. Scientists are constantly coming up with new ideas. In the meantime, we can still count on gravity to keep our feet on the ground. **We just can't completely explain why.**

Earth's invisible gravitational force pulls the meteorite away from its path and towards Earth.

No, this is what really happens. The meteorite is still following the straightest path through space, but space itself has been bent out of shape by Earth!

What is the speed of dark?

Darkness is just a lack of light. When an object blocks the path of light, we get darkness. So to measure the speed of dark, we need to know **how fast light travels**. Scientists have measured the speed of light, and it's FAST. **So fast** that if you stand on one side of the room and turn a torch on, the light travelling from the bulb seems to reach the other side of the room straight away. We don't notice any delay until we are further away – a LOT further away! Even if you stood on the Moon and switched on a very bright torch, people back on Earth would see the light just 1.3 seconds later. **Light is the fastest thing** in the universe. Now let's create some darkness, by putting your hand in front of the torch and blocking its light. If you did this, a shadow would fall over Earth 1.3 seconds later, just after the last bit of light from the torch reached the Earth. So in a way, we can think of darkness as having the same speed as light. Next time you're feeling a bit ***nervous*** **of the** ***dark***, just remember you can switch on a light and make the dark disappear faster than ANYTHING else in the universe!

How does Earth float in space?

In photographs, Earth looks like it's floating in space. But **our planet is actually falling towards the Sun,** because of the Sun's **huge** gravitational force. Don't worry though – Earth will never get any closer to the Sun! This *sounds* impossible, but we can understand how it works by playing with tennis balls. Imagine gently hitting a tennis ball. It zooms forwards for a bit, then falls towards the ground because of Earth's gravity. If you drew the path of the ball in the air, it would be a curved shape. Now hit the ball harder. It travels further before gravity brings it down to the ground. The path is still a curved shape. Now imagine you could hit the ball so hard that it speeds away at 28,800 km per hour! The ball would still begin to fall, just as it did before, but this time **it would never hit the ground.** Its curved path would exactly match the curve of Earth's surface, so the ball would keep falling all the way around the world! This is basically how we put things into orbit around Earth. Instead of using a tennis racket, we use a rocket to get satellites and astronauts travelling fast enough. In the same way, Earth is moving sideways compared to the Sun, but it's moving so quickly that it falls all the way around the Sun once every year. We don't notice being on this **cosmic rollercoaster,** because we too are falling around the Sun at exactly the same speed as our planet!

How do we know Earth is round?

Photographs snapped from space show that our planet is a giant ball of rock, water and gas. That's the short answer, but it took a long time to get to it. After all, it doesn't *feel* like we're walking around on a sphere. Like ants on a watermelon, we're **too small** to notice the ground curving away. It was the ancient Greeks who first worked out the truth. They spent a lot of time thinking about things and loved nothing better than an impossible question. Greek astronomers noticed that Earth casts a **round** shadow on the Moon during a lunar eclipse, and that the bottom of a ship is the first thing to **disappear over the horizon** as it sails away. If Earth was flat, the whole ship would just get smaller and smaller, until it became a dot. The bottom of a ship could only disappear first if Earth's surface was curved.

The ancient Greeks also noticed that the midday Sun appears lower in the sky the further north you go. If Earth was flat, the Sun would be the same height above the horizon no matter where you stood. One ancient Greek astronomer used this information to work out Earth's circumference! Not everyone believed the **strange truth** straight away, even when ships set sail heading west, sailed all the way around the planet, and arrived back home from the east! When space travel began in the 1950s, humans finally saw Earth for themselves. But we've also discovered that it's not *perfectly* round. Our planet spins so quickly, it's a little flatter at the poles and a little bulged in the middle – **rather like a watermelon!**

The circumference is the distance all the way around.

How long would it take to go all the way around the world?

It's impossible to give you just one answer. It depends who (or what) is travelling, and how! Astronauts orbiting Earth in the International Space Station zoom all the way around the world in just 90 minutes, but they're **flying** about 400 km above Earth's surface, travelling almost 8 km every second! Closer to the ground, the big blanket of air around Earth slows a flying object down – **just like walking through water slows you down**. The fastest flight around the equator (the fattest part of our ball-shaped planet) took 31 hours, 27 minutes and 49 seconds – that was in a **supersonic plane**! Giant birds called albatrosses have made the same journey in just 46 days, but without jet engines to help!

Down on Earth's surface, both humans and animals move even more slowly. Walking around the planet would take almost a year, even if it was possible to walk non-stop **without loo-breaks or sleep!** Most people use some kind of vehicle, and the distance travelled depends on where their journey starts and ends. The very first circumnavigation (journey around the world) was by ship and took three years. That voyage happened 500 years ago, and boats today are a lot faster! The fastest-ever boat trip around the world took just 40 days, 23 hours and 30 minutes. People like to break records, so we can expect **even speedier** journeys in the future. **Perhaps you will make one yourself!** But don't worry if you'd rather stay put. Earth is constantly spinning on its axis, so just by sitting still you actually travel all the way around the centre of our planet and back to where you started once every 24 hours!

Why am I me and not someone else?

Think about all the things that make you unique. Not just the way you look (which helps your friends and family spot you in a crowd), but try thinking about your likes and dislikes …

LIKES

DISLIKES

You're not just one in a million. You're one in 7.7 billion, and counting! It's impossible to say EXACTLY what makes you *you*. Your **genome** is part of the answer. This is like an **instruction manual** from your parents, which your body follows as it grows and develops. It guides how your body looks and also how it works. If these instructions were written down as a string of letters, the genome would be **3 billion letters long** – that's enough information to fill 16,000 books like this one! Our bodies are following the instructions in our genome when they grow two ears, a stomach, one nose and ten toes.

Our genome is what makes us grow into humans rather than starfish, daffodils or mice. Those living things all have different genomes. But human genomes are also a little different from each other. If you compared your genome with the genome of your best friend, you'd spot around **5 million small differences.** That sounds like a lot, but it's actually a tiny number in a list of 3 billion letters. So our genomes alone can't explain all the differences between us.

Scientists have discovered that the human genome is fairly 'plastic'. This doesn't mean that it's made of plastic, but that it's a bit **squidgy and flexible**. It means that many of the instructions in our genome are just a starting point for **who we are going to become**. Our bodies can follow these instructions in a variety of ways, depending on all the different things we experience as we grow and develop. Everything you've ever seen, heard, smelled, done, touched, drunk and eaten is part of your environment – the second big thing that shapes the person you are. Your genome and environment often work closely together. For example, your genome makes it **possible** for you to learn languages by telling your body how to build a brain, ears, eyes, hands and a mouth. But the actual languages you know depend on your environment – where you grow up, who is around and what you learn at school. Often, it's impossible to say exactly how much of a particular feature is thanks to your genome, and how much is thanks to your environment. But you can be certain that you're **the only person in the whole history** of the world to combine your genome AND your life experiences. **That's what makes you YOU instead of someone else.**

Our flexible, 'plastic' genomes allow us to learn and cope with new challenges and experiences that our ancestors didn't face.

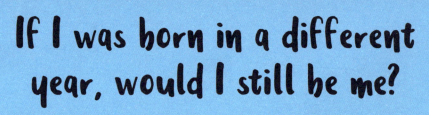

If I was born in a different year, would I still be me?

No, because you would have a different genome AND a different environment. Let's start with your genome. You get this instruction manual from your parents. But the information included isn't always copied across exactly – it's more **like a pick 'n' mix**, where each birth parent supplies roughly half of the sweets in the bag! The pick 'n' mix process is complicated (imagine a choice of 84,000 sweets but only 21,000 fit in the bag!). **The chances of picking the exact same set of sweets twice are tiny.** Even if it did happen, your environment would be **different in thousands of ways** if you were born in a different year. Your parents would be different ages. You would meet different teachers and friends at school. You might eat different foods and form different opinions. The only people who are born with identical genomes are identical twins. They often grow up in similar environments too. But identical twins are still totally different people because no set of experiences is ever exactly the same. So it's possible to say that if you were born in a different year, you wouldn't be you. **But then who would you be?** Well that's an *impossible* question!

Why can't I remember being a baby?

Don't worry, you're not the only one! Most people can't remember anything about their first few years on the planet. At the moment it's hard to explain why we forget **so much.** Our brains are good at remembering skills we learn as babies. We don't forget how to walk, talk, or recognise our families. Three-year-olds can remember all kinds of things. But by the time we are seven, most events and experiences that happened before we were three have been **mysteriously wiped from our brains!** Scientists have come up with different theories to explain this. One idea is that **we can't store memories** until we learn enough language to turn them into 'stories'. Another idea is that a child's brain **grows and changes** so quickly, that new brain cells and connections mess up the memories that are already there. Even older children and adults seem to forget experiences quickly, unless they are very important or make us feel very strong feelings.

What experiences do you remember from when you were very young? Why are they important to you? Why not draw or write them down, to help you remember them forever!

If you're younger than seven you will probably forget this page in the future, so be sure to come back and read it again!

Why don't caterpillars get stung by nettles?

Ow! Plants might look pretty and peaceful from a distance, but some of them are packed with **powerful poisons**. They can't run away from enemies, so they have to rely on **devious defences**. Nettles are covered in tiny, brittle hairs that break easily when we brush against them (they're actually made of the same stuff as glass!). As the broken tip scratches our skin, chemicals rush up through the hollow hair and **deliver a nasty sting**. It's a cunning defence that keeps away hungry herbivores, like sheep and deer. So it's confusing that dozens of butterflies and moths love to lay their eggs on nettle plants. When their caterpillars hatch, they happily tuck into leaves that would send a human running for the first aid kit!

So far it's been impossible to tell if these caterpillars are **immune** to the stings, or if they are simply putting up with the pain. Perhaps they're just really good at crawling past the hairs without breaking them (being small probably helps). Whichever theory is correct, it seems that nettles have adapted to stop BIG herbivores from grazing but are happier to host smaller critters – including pollinators, and insects that provide food for birds and other animals. So next time you get stung, don't take it out on the nettles. **A friend to insects is also a friend to us!**

In the UK, more than 100 insects and other creepy-crawlies can be seen feeding on nettles. In one experiment, snails feasted just as happily on normal nettle leaves as they did when the stinging hairs were shaved off!

Why do insects have six legs?

How many different insects can you think of? Enormous, multi-coloured moths. Shiny black beetles. Strange-looking stick insects. Armies of ants. There are **more than a million** types of insect, and they are different from one another in so many ways. But they all have six legs. **Why not two or four?** Why not 100 or more?

Fossils show us that the ancestors of insects have had six legs for about 400 million years! This tells us that being a hexapod (a six-legged creature) must be **very helpful** to insects. If a feature is not helpful, it tends to disappear over time – for example, fish and other animals that spend their entire lives in pitch-black caves have adapted by not bothering to grow eyes. It's impossible to know for sure why six legs has proved to be so helpful, but one idea is that six legs make it easier for insects to balance as they walk. Smaller things lose their **balance** more quickly – try balancing a small pencil and a big stick on a fingertip to see for yourself! If you film an insect walking and watch it in slow motion, you'll see that it walks by lifting three legs at once (two legs on one side and the middle leg on the other). This always leaves three feet on the ground, which stops it tipping over. Other animals such as crabs and springtails have six legs too. Scientists are even copying these hexapods to design robots that can cross rough ground without falling over. These robo-animals could soon be carrying out **daring rescues** on Earth, or even **exploring other worlds**.

How do bubbles work?

If you looked at water under a **very, very powerful microscope,** you'd see it is made up of gazillions of miniscule molecules. These molecules love to cling to each other – this is why water on a wet window clumps together in drops. If you dip a bubble wand into pure water, the water left on the wand clings together in a big drop too. Adding soap to water makes the molecules a little less clingy. If you dip a bubble wand into soapy water, the molecules hold on to each other *just enough* to form **a shimmering, soapy wall.** When you **blow air** at this wall, you start a competition between the force of the air (which is trying to pull the molecules apart) and the force with which the water molecules cling to each other. At first the soapy wall s t r e t c h e s. Then a little dimple forms. The dimple gets bigger and fills with air. Finally, the water molecules right at the bottom of the dimple **snap** together, trapping the air inside. The bubble floats away, carrying those **mucilaginous** molecules on a new adventure!

Mucilaginous means something sticky or gloopy.

Why are bubbles always round?

You can use a bubble wand shaped like a heart, square or star, but the bubbles always end up ball-shaped. Even if you blow a gigantic, wonky bubble, it will **wibble and wobble** as it tries to reshape itself into a sphere. You're actually watching an epic battle of different forces! The air trapped inside the bubble is made of molecules too, but they don't cling together like molecules of water. In fact, **they try to move apart!** They push against the inside of the bubble's soapy wall, trying to break the water molecules apart. But the molecules of soapy water refuse to be separated! They cling on to each other, pushing back on the air. They can do this more easily if they arrange themselves into the **smallest possible** shape. This is a sphere, or ball shape, where each water molecule clings to its neighbours with the same force. On Earth, there's a third force at work – gravity – which can make big bubbles bottom heavy. But in space (or microgravity) bubbles are perfect spheres. Once a bubble is in this shape, the forces are balanced, and the battle is over … at least until a new force manages to pull those water molecules apart … and the bubble … POPS!

Why do children have to go to bed so early?

Sleep is mysterious. We don't know exactly why we need to sleep, but we do know it's **very important for survival.** In fact, it's so important that EVERY OTHER ANIMAL sleeps too. Even jellyfish try to catch up on any sleep they miss! This tells us that the benefits of sleep are worth the risk of being less alert to sharks creeping up on you. **Sleep is a special kind of rest,** when our bodies are less active than usual. Our eyelids close and almost all our muscles go floppy. Some parts of our brain get a break – we stop seeing, hearing and smelling things, so we don't have to think about them. But, for some reason, other parts of our brain seem to work even harder than usual. We still don't know exactly what's going on in there – **human brains are the most complicated things in the universe to understand!** But scientists think our sleeping brains could be hard at work making new brain cells, storing memories, practising new skills we have learned, and even giving themselves a good clean!

The amount of time your brain needs to get all these jobs done changes as you get older. When you are young, you are **growing and learning** very quickly, so you need more sleep. From ages three to five, you need up to 13 hours of sleep every night. School-age children need up to 11 hours of sleep. If you get enough sleep you will feel alert the next day. **If you miss out on sleep,** your brain might find it hard to concentrate, solve problems and make decisions. It just wants to catch up on sleep. **This can make you feel very moody.** Teenagers need a little less sleep than younger children, and adults only need 7 to 9 hours each night. In a family, often everyone needs to wake up at the same time, to go to work and school. So going to bed earlier than adults is the best way for children (and jellyfish) to make sure they get enough sleep, and keep their brains happy!

Can I sleep with my eyes open?

If only Sleeping Beauty had fallen asleep for **100 years** with her eyes wide open. She could have watched TV the ENTIRE time she was stuck in the castle! In real life, most of us sleep with our eyes **tightly shut**. A few animals (such as ducks and dolphins) CAN sleep with one eye open. This is possible because just half of their brain falls asleep at a time. It means snoozing dolphins can still swim up to the surface of the ocean to breathe, and sleeping ducks can spot foxes hunting for a midnight feast. **Some sea birds can even fly for miles while they doze.** But unless you happen to be a duck or a dolphin, you'll have to close your eyes to get to sleep. It might seem **boring** to spend so much time in the dark, but it keeps tears in and dust out, so your eyes stay healthy. It even gives your tears a chance to kill nasty germs overnight. And it gives a big part of your brain a break. **Darkness** is so good at **helping our brains fall asleep,** it's hard to stay awake when your eyes are closed. Even when you blink, your brain takes a tiny nap – even though the darkness lasts less than a second! You blink at least 30,000 times every day, which is a lot of extra naps! The real question is, **is it possible to stay awake when my eyes are closed?**

Why doesn't gravity work on balloons?

Most objects fall to the ground if you drop them, but some party balloons seem to follow different rules. If you let go of a helium-filled balloon it moves UP! Earth's gravitational force does work on helium balloons, pulling every particle DOWN towards the ground. But this pull is cancelled out by another force pushing the balloon up. It's the same type of force that makes things float in water. A helium balloon is also floating … in air.

Think of a rubber duck held at the bottom of a bath. To be there, it has to push a duck-shaped amount of water out of the way, and **that water pushes back!** This push is called the buoyant force. The more water that gets pushed out of the way, the bigger the buoyant force. For a rubber duck that's completely underwater, the push of the buoyant force is much greater than the pull of gravity – so **as soon as you let go,** the duck starts moving up. Once it reaches the surface, less of the duck is underwater so it's pushing less water out of the way. The buoyant force is now exactly the SAME SIZE as the downwards pull caused by gravity, the two forces cancel each other out and the duck floats. We can predict which objects will float, rather than sink – it's the ones that weigh less than the amount of water they push out of the way. An air-filled rubber duck weighs less than a rubber-duck shaped amount of water, so it will float.

Similarly, the gas helium is far lighter than air, so a helium-filled balloon weighs less than the air it pushes out of the way. This means the buoyant force of the air is big enough to overcome the force of gravity and push the balloon upwards. Just like the duck in the bath, **a helium balloon will keep moving up** until the air around it becomes so thin, the weight of the air pushed aside by the balloon matches the weight of the balloon – **or until the balloon pops!** This usually happens first because party balloons tend to pop at around 10 km above Earth's surface. The helium escapes and keeps moving up, but gravity will pull the empty balloon back down

down

down

to Earth.

What's that floating thing?

Can birds fly to space if they want?

Birds don't float in air like balloons. They overcome the pull of gravity with a different kind of push. Flapping wings pull in air and push it downwards, away from the bird's body. The air pushes back on the bird equally hard, creating an upwards force called lift! The bigger the bird, the **bigger** the wings needed to produce the right amount of lift to overcome gravity. Some birds use a different trick to create lift. They open very long wings over rising warm air, which pushes them upwards. But even GIGANTIC wings couldn't carry a bird all the way into space. The higher you get above Earth's surface, the thinner the air, which means there is less oxygen to breathe. Small birds can fly to a height of about 5,000 m, where the air has about half the oxygen that it has at sea level. Some birds have bodies that can cope with even less oxygen. A Rüppell's griffon vulture has been spotted more than 11 km up! But even if one of these high-flying vultures wore a tiny spacesuit (with room for a beak), it still couldn't flap its way up into space. Soon the air becomes **so thin** that it's impossible to generate lift. So a Rüppell's griffon vulture may be able to peer into the windows of a jumbo jet, but it's still a long way from being an astronaut. Space officially starts ten times further up, 100 km off the ground!

No need to get in such a flap!

How do aeroplanes fly?

This question has proved impossible to answer for more than **100 years**! Engineers have designed planes that can **loop the loop**, aircraft with a wingspan as long as a **football pitch**, and jumbo jets with room for **850 passengers** at once. But they still disagree about exactly HOW these planes stay up in the air!

Here are the things we do know:

Air needs to move around the wings for an aeroplane to fly.

This means a plane has to be moving quickly to take off and stay up in the air – the engines provide this forwards force, called thrust.

The special curved shape of the wings is important (it even has a name – an aerofoil).

An upwards force called lift cancels out the downwards force caused by gravity.

Here's the thing we don't know:

Where this lift comes from!

There are two leading ideas, or theories. **The first idea** comes from looking carefully at how air flows around the wings of a plane. By flowing smoky air over a fake wing, we can see that air moves faster over the top of the wing than the bottom. It's also more spread out than the air below the wing. Perhaps the bunched-up air underneath presses harder on the bottom of the wing than the spread-out air on top, and the difference is what creates the LIFT that makes a plane go up **and stay up**! However, this CAN'T explain why some planes can fly perfectly well upside down.

The second idea is that the curved shape of the wing constantly pushes air downwards. The air pushes back and so the wing (and the plane attached to it) are pushed up. This is a bit like the upwards push people feel if they hold their hand out of a car window when they're whizzing along. However, this CAN'T explain why the air is more spread out on top of the wing, or the effect this has.

Each idea is good, but neither can completely explain lift on its own. The answer is probably a mixture of all these things: the downwards flow of air, the speed of air above the wing, AND the difference in pressure. So until someone works out how to combine all these things into one neat explanation, the puzzle of how some of the world's heaviest vehicles stay up in the sky remains **impossible to solve**.

Lift

Thrust

Drag

Gravity

Overcoming gravity is only half the problem ... a plane also needs to overcome drag, a force that slows moving objects down as they rub against the air. Engineers try to make drag as small as possible by giving aeroplanes a smooth shape, but they still gobble up huge amounts of fuel to keep flying fast enough to generate lift.

Why don't animals wear clothes?

Animals in storybooks are often very well dressed, but in real life we never see weasels wearing waistcoats or toads looking terrific in tweed. No matter how cold it gets, badgers never slip on a pair of woolly socks. At first glance, **humans seem to be the only animals that wear clothes.** It's impossible to say when – or why – this began. One idea is that our ancestors needed clothes to **keep them warm,** as they gradually lost the fur that covers other mammals. But dolphins don't have much fur either and you'll never spot one of them in a wetsuit. Another idea is that clothes allowed humans to **migrate from Africa,** where the first humans lived, to colder parts of the world. But clothes do much more than simply keeping us warm or dry. We use clothes to tell other people something about ourselves – which groups or teams we belong to, which music, films and fashions we like, or even how we are feeling.

Amazingly, there ARE **other animals that decorate themselves too** – especially animals that live in water! Decorator crabs have shells covered in tiny hooks that work a bit like Velcro, letting them stick corals, seaweed or sponges to their shells. This seems to help them **hide** from predators. Some hermit crabs even accessorize with sea anemones **to stop themselves getting attacked!** Sea urchins also cover themselves with rocks, shells and scraps of seaweed, perhaps to protect themselves from the Sun, just as we would put on a T-shirt to play on the beach. Young caddisflies actually make their own armour, using silk to glue twigs, sand and gravel together.

On land, tiny insects called lacewings dress themselves up in a mixture of their own droppings, and a waxy 'wool' made from the bodies of aphids! This **gruesome costume** seems to shield them from attacks by wasps, ladybirds and ants. Assassin bugs sometimes carry a backpack made from **dead ants**, which makes them look less delicious to spiders, geckos and centipedes. Even some rodents have been seen sticking **old snake skins** to their fur … perhaps to discourage snakes from eating them. All of these animals are not just trying to keep warm, they're trying to change their appearance. This is a big clue about why humans wear clothes. Luckily, we can choose trousers, dresses and T-shirts rather than dead insects or animal droppings!

I think I'll stick with what I'm wearing!

Why are puppies cute?

Some animals, such as snakes, never meet their offspring. Others spend months or even years looking after their young. Scientists think that **cuteness** may be a feature of **baby animals** in the second group! Fossils show us that even certain baby dinosaurs had big eyes and huge heads compared to their body size. Cute looks may help to make animal parents think "I want to look after you" instead of "I want to eat you!" But when it comes to puppies it's not just other dogs that find them adorable – **plenty of humans do too!** Those big, round eyes. Those soft, floppy ears. That cute button nose! Is it because puppies remind us of human babies (the large heads and eyes, not the floppy ears)? Or could it be something else?

In one of the most ADORABLE experiments ever carried out, scientists asked people to look at pictures of puppies. They found out that puppies look cutest to humans when they are about eight weeks old. This is the same age that puppies stop drinking their mother's milk and start to rely on US to feed them. Perhaps puppies have adapted to look cute so that **humans want to look after them!** After all, most dogs are no longer wild animals. We have kept them as pets and working dogs for hundreds of years. If humans typically pick the cutest puppies to care for, and those cute puppies grow up to have cute puppies of their own, then over hundreds of years puppies would have become **cuter and cuter!**

Of course, this can't explain why humans find baby pandas, seahorses and tigers so loveable. What's the cutest baby animal you've ever seen?

Do wasps know that they hurt people when they sting?

When we ask this question, we are really asking – do insects think in the same way we do? Does a wasp sting because it's angry you licked that spoon clean of jam, and wants to get its own back? Or is it more like a nettle, which stings without ever knowing? Wasps can't tell us the answer, no matter how nicely we ask. So scientists look for clues instead. When we swat a wasp away from our picnic, and it swoops straight back again, we imagine that it feels annoyed! Humans have big brains and big imaginations, which allow us to put ourselves in another person's (or a wasp's) shoes. But does a wasp's brain work in the same way? Can a wasp put itself in human shoes, imagine the pain that we might feel when it stings us, and plan to launch an attack?

An insect's brain might be tiny compared to a human brain, but wasps do many things that seem super smart. They live in big groups, divide up work between themselves, and can learn to tell different wasps apart. They seem to have a range of emotions too. For example, a wasp that is trapped inside a window behaves differently to a wasp that is looking for food. Over and over again, it walks up the glass, drops down, then walks back up again. To us, the wasp seems angry and anxious to find a way out. But perhaps it's just following a pattern that works well for getting around obstacles outdoors – flying up and towards the light. A wasp might respond to certain triggers in the environment – like a huge, swatting hand – by stinging, without actually feeling anger. It's impossible to say for sure, because we don't know enough about what goes on inside a wasp's brain. But we can keep putting ourselves in their shoes, and count on them turning up to as many picnics as we do.

Why do we need eyebrows?

Humans have far less hair than most other mammals, except for whales and dolphins. So why do our bodies still **go to the trouble of growing a caterpillar of hair** above each eye? To find possible answers, scientists think about how bushy brows may have helped our ancestors. Perhaps they **shaded their eyes from the Sun** – all the better for spotting sabre-toothed tigers! Perhaps they **soaked up sweat** or rain that trickled down smooth foreheads. Or perhaps we held on to our eyebrows for a different reason – to show other people how we are feeling! **Sometimes, eyebrows can speak louder than words.** See if you can work out how these emojis are feeling:

Muscles under your skin can pull your eyebrows into all sorts of shapes, from furrowing in a frown, to arching in surprise. For our ancestors this would have been particularly helpful. Ancient humans began living in groups long before they developed complicated languages. Being able to 'read' someone's face and tell if they were angry or worried, happy or sad would have helped people to **work together and survive.** We still give and read these signals all the time, without thinking about it. For example, most people quickly raise their eyebrows when they see someone approaching – a **secret signal** that we mean them no harm. Our eyebrows are probably doing the same job as a dog's wagging tail. **We have eyebrows to help us make friends**!

Eyebrows may even help humans to recognise each other. In one experiment, people found it easier to recognise a face with hidden EYES than hidden eyebrows!

Why do we cry?

Just above each eye, between your eyelashes and eyebrow, lies a **hidden tear factory**. These lacrimal glands work hard to make **three different types of tears**. The first type are in your eyes all the time, forming a thin, shiny, see-through layer that helps you to see properly, and constantly washes dust and pollen out of your eyes. A typical person releases 10 to 20 tablespoons of these tears EVERY DAY! Over a year, that would be **enough to fill a large bath**. Luckily, they don't collect in one place – they are constantly flowing across your eyes and draining out through tiny tubes into your nose. The second type of tears are thin and watery, made to wash away anything that could harm your eyes … including the tiny, stinky particles that escape into the air when someone chops an onion! They are the type of tears you shed when an insect flies into your eye (the insect would be crying too, if it could!).

The third type of tears are the **most mysterious**. They can start to flow when we are feeling sad, disappointed or angry, or even when we're feeling happy. Our eyes make **so many** of these tears that there's no time for them all to drain away into our nose. They spill over our eyelids and run down our cheeks. Humans are the **only animals that seem to cry these emotional tears**, and in the past, people have come up with lots of ideas to try and explain why. However, the biggest clue comes from the tears themselves. Emotional tears are different from onion tears. They seem to contain more proteins that make them 'stick' to our faces for longer, making them easier for other people to spot! The best explanation is that **tears do a similar job to our eyebrows** – they help us to show other people how we feel, hopefully bringing help and comfort. There's still another impossible question to answer though – why do some people cry easily, while others spend their whole lives hardly shedding any tears at all?

> Have you heard the phrase 'crocodile tears'? Crocodiles really do cry – but only when they eat. These tears seem to be a side effect of their hissing and huffing – not because they're having a bad day! No animals have been seen crying emotional tears.

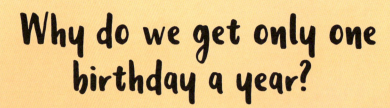

Why do we get only one birthday a year?

Humans could have chosen to throw birthday parties every 7, 30 or 84 days. **So why pick 365?** You can blame the ancient Egyptians! They were some of the first people to notice that **the Sun and stars follow a pattern**, appearing in the same places in the sky roughly every 365 days. The Egyptians didn't know it at the time, but the patterns they noticed are caused by our planet's orbit around the Sun – a journey that takes 365 and a quarter days (one year). They began **celebrating important festivals** – like the birthdays of kings and queens – once a year, guided by the stars. The ancient Romans went a step further. They created calendars and celebrated the birthdays of ordinary folk as well as Very Important People. One of these ancient party invitations was found written on a scrap of wood left behind at Hadrian's Wall! Like us, the Romans had cake at their birthday parties, but the person whose birthday it was **gave** the gifts! Perhaps that's why they felt once a year was enough. You could argue that every WEEK you are on the planet is something worth celebrating, but it's pretty cool that each birthday marks another trip all the way around the Sun.

How long would it take to count to infinity?

Try counting up to ten by saying each number out loud:

1, 2, 3, 4, 5, 6, 7, 8, 9, 10 ...

How long did it take? If you kept going and counted one number every second (without ever stopping to sleep), it would take you about 11 and a half days to count up to a million. Counting to a billion would take almost **32 years**. And counting to a trillion would take almost **32,000 years**! But even if you were an immortal robot calculator that could keep counting forever, it would be **impossible to count to infinity**. Infinity is not a number – it's just a way to describe something that goes on forever. The 'natural numbers' that we count with are infinite. No matter how large a number you think of, you could always add one more. **And it's impossible to count up to the end of something that goes on forever**. Luckily, we don't need to. If we know it's possible to say every number, but that there is **no end** to these numbers, then as soon as we start to count we are technically counting to(wards) infinity!

12520 ...
12519,
12518,
12517,
12516,
12515,
12514,
12513,
12512,
12511,
12510,
12509,
12508,
12507,
12506,
12505,

180 ...
179,
178,
177,
176,
175,
174,
173, 172, 171, 170, 169, 168, 167, 166, 165, 164, 163, 162,

How many stars are there?

Gazing up at space on a dark night, it feels like there are too many stars to possibly count. But people have tried. On a **moonless night** in the countryside, human eyes can detect light from several thousand of the very brightest stars. With the help of binoculars, we can see light from much further and fainter stars – up to **200,000** of them. And with a small telescope, we can see millions! So how many stars are there altogether? This is impossible to answer. **Even with the most powerful telescopes, only part of the universe is visible from Earth**. We can't count stars that we can't see. But we can estimate – or make a best guess – using the evidence we do have.

The highest estimates suggest the universe contains around **a trillion, trillion (1,000,000,000,000,000,000,000,000) stars**. This number is amazing, but it's probably wrong! Estimating is difficult, because stars aren't spread evenly through space, but clumped together in big groups called galaxies. Our galaxy, the Milky Way, is thought to contain at least **100 billion stars**, but we can't even be sure of this. Learning more about the Milky Way should help us to make better estimates about the entire universe, but we'll never know for sure how many stars there are. **The universe is unimaginably vast**, and is constantly changing as **old stars die**, and **new stars flicker into life**. Look up at the stars this evening. How many can you count?

How big is the universe?

Earth might look pretty big from where you're standing, but our planet is but a speck of dust in a universe so enormous that just thinking about it is guaranteed to boggle your brain! We can measure the distance to nearby cosmic objects, such as the Moon or Mars, by sending out a beam of radio waves, and timing how long it takes the beam to bounce off these space rocks and back to Earth. We know how fast radio waves travel through space, so we can work out the distance they have travelled in that time. Measuring the distance to distant stars and galaxies is harder, because most of them are further away than radio waves can travel in a human lifetime. But if we look closely enough, there are clues hidden in the light that has travelled to Earth from those distant objects. For example, the closer a star is to us, the brighter it appears. By studying the light from stars, we've worked out our galaxy – the Milky Way – is about 120,000 light years across. A light year is the distance that light can travel in one year and it's a HUGE distance, because light moves VERY quickly. It works out at 1,140 quadrillion km from one side of the Milky Way to the other! In a family car going at top speed on a motorway, this journey would take a trillion years.

You should definitely stop for a loo break before you leave the Milky Way, because the next nearest large galaxy, Andromeda, is around 2.5 million light years away – that's another 21 trillion years in a car! But even this is close compared to the very furthest galaxies that telescopes can see – thought to be a whopping 46.5 billion light years from Earth. If we can see 46.5 billion light years in every direction, this tells us the universe must be at least 93 billion light years across. It doesn't stop there, but the problem is, we can't see any further than this. The light from stars and galaxies more than 46.5 billion light years away simply hasn't had time to reach us yet! Some space scientists have estimated that the entire universe is up to 250 times bigger than the part we can see! We'll never be able to measure the whole universe, but there is one thing we do know for sure: the parts we can see are more than big enough to keep even the most intrepid explorer busy.

Are aliens real?

It's impossible to answer yes, because no one has even seen an alien. But it's impossible to answer no, because we haven't yet looked on (or under) every rock in the universe! **Here's what we do know**: our Sun is not the only star that is orbited by planets. In fact, scientists estimate there's an average of one such planet – or exoplanet – orbiting EVERY star in the universe! Space is so unimaginably vast, it's very likely that in galaxies far, far away, all sorts of aliens are happily going about their lives. **So where should we look first**?

That looks too hot!

That looks too cold!

That looks just right!

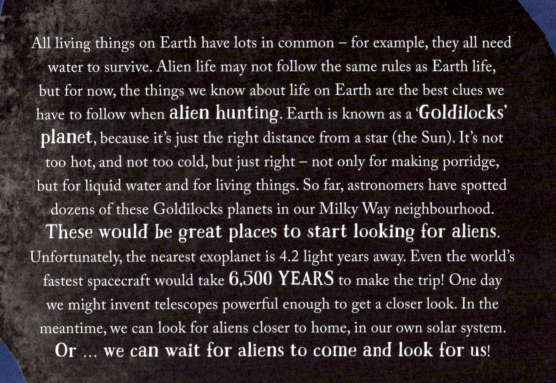

All living things on Earth have lots in common – for example, they all need water to survive. Alien life may not follow the same rules as Earth life, but for now, the things we know about life on Earth are the best clues we have to follow when **alien hunting**. Earth is known as a 'Goldilocks' **planet**, because it's just the right distance from a star (the Sun). It's not too hot, and not too cold, but just right – not only for making porridge, but for liquid water and for living things. So far, astronomers have spotted dozens of these Goldilocks planets in our Milky Way neighbourhood. **These would be great places to start looking for aliens.** Unfortunately, the nearest exoplanet is 4.2 light years away. Even the world's fastest spacecraft would take **6,500 YEARS** to make the trip! One day we might invent telescopes powerful enough to get a closer look. In the meantime, we can look for aliens closer to home, in our own solar system. **Or ... we can wait for aliens to come and look for us!**

Nearby planets and moons may look lifeless in photographs, but so do many deserts and mountains on Earth – until you flip over the right rocks! Future probes and rovers sent to explore our solar system will be able to flip over more and more rocks, and may discover aliens living **closer than we thought ...**

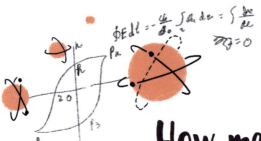

How many atoms are there in my body?

Atoms are the **building blocks of everything in the universe**, including our bodies. They are so small, that if you magnified an atom to the size of an apple, and magnified the apple by the same amount, **you'd end up with an apple the size of Earth**! It's impossible to count the atoms in a human one by one, but we can make a sensible guess. We can weigh an atom and work out how many atoms add up to the weight of a human. This isn't as simple as it sounds, because there are more than **90 different types** of atoms (known as elements) and each one has a **different weight**. So, first, we need to know which atoms humans are made of. It turns out that a human body is mostly made of hydrogen, oxygen and carbon atoms. Crunching the numbers tells us that a 10-year-old child weighing 45 kg (7 stone) is made of about … (drumroll) …

4,500,000,000,000,000,000,000,000,000 (4.5 octillion) atoms!

These atoms aren't just piled up in a **human-shaped heap**. They are organised into millions of different molecules, which do all the different jobs in your body. Every time you pull out an eyelash, chew off a fingernail or pick your nose, you lose trillions of atoms. But don't worry – every drink, breath and meal tops you up with trillions more!

What are atoms made from?

For 2,000 years, atoms were thought to be the smallest building blocks of everything. The word atom even **means 'impossible to cut up'**. But around a hundred years ago, scientists realised that atoms could be split into *even smaller* particles, which were named protons, neutrons and electrons. Inside each atom, these particles are arranged a bit like a teeny tiny solar system. At its centre is a clump of heavy protons and neutrons – particles so small **you could line up a trillion of each on the full stop at the end of this sentence.** This clump is known as the 'nucleus' of the atom. It's orbited by a cloud of even smaller electrons. Finding out that atoms were made from these three types of particles has helped scientists to explain some of the stranger things about the universe, such as electricity (which is just electrons on the move).

To learn more about atoms, scientists built machines called particle accelerators that can **smash particles** into each other at enormous speeds. They discovered that it is possible to break protons and neutrons up into **even tinier particles**, known as quarks. Like electrons, quarks are so tiny they almost seem to have no size at all. We still have **lots to learn** about quarks and electrons, but at the moment they seem to be the smallest particles of all – and the building blocks of all the atoms in the universe.

Do animals have imaginations?

Imagination is the way we **build different worlds** inside our heads. We use our imaginations when we read and write stories and paint pictures. Animals don't do these things (or not that we've noticed)! But we also use our imaginations when we plan a birthday party, invent a toy that doesn't exist, or worry about speaking in front of the class. The worlds we build inside our heads **help us to plan** for things that might happen, instead of just reacting to what is happening right now. Some animals DO seem to be able to do this, and funnily enough, most of them are birds.

Our first brainy birds are **Western scrub jays**. They aren't as cute as they look. One of their habits is **stealing food** that has been collected by other jays! After doing this once, they seem to be able to imagine other jays doing the same to them. If they spot another jay watching them hide food, **they will go back and move it later**. Just like a person hiding chocolates from the rest of their family, the jays are using old memories to predict something that might happen in the future – then planning ahead!

New Caledonian crows are also brilliant at planning ahead! In one experiment, the crows were given a box filled with **yummy food,** and a selection of tools. The only way to get to the food was by using a long, thin stick, but this was one tool they **didn't have**. They didn't give up. Half of the crows managed to invent and build the right kind of tool, using the materials they had. **They must have been using imagination**! So far, these brainy birds are some of the best evidence we have that animals really do have imaginations. And studying bird behaviour isn't just interesting for animal experts. It may help us to better understand how our own amazing imaginations work.

Mmmm, there's my dinner.

I know what you're planning.

Why are there so many different types of living things?

Scientists think that Earth is home to around **8.7 million** different types of plants, animals, fungi and other living things. Throughout history, people have tried to explain how they all got here. The answer was found by looking very closely at nature and **piecing together the clues.** We can find all these clues by peering into a pond full of tadpoles …

Clue 1

There's only a certain amount of food, water and shelter in the pond – not enough for all these tadpoles! **There are also some predators** that like to eat tadpoles (can you spot them?).

This means that … it's sad, **but not all the tadpoles will survive** to become adult frogs. It's the same with the seeds on a dandelion or the acorns on an oak tree. Most living things have more offspring than can possibly survive.

When you put these facts together, they explain how creatures adapt to their habitats over time. At first, the new group of tadpoles might not be that different from last year's group – just a few more tadpoles with longer tails. **But imagine the same process going on for hundreds, thousands or even MILLIONS of years.** Eventually, the tadpoles in this pond may be so different from tadpoles living in other ponds that they have become an entirely different type of animal!

This explains HOW different types of living things come about, but **why so many**? Well, the first living things appeared on Earth about 3.8 BILLION years ago. Since then, they have been moving around and **adapting to millions of different habitats** all over the world. As they became better adapted to the habitats they found themselves in, they became less and less like their ancestors. Over billions of years, tiny changes have added up to the **BIG differences** we see today – the differences between a polar bear and a palm tree, between a newt and a gnat, or between a penguin and a person!

Clue 2

The tadpoles aren't exactly the same as each other. There are **lots of small differences**, such as the length of their tails. We call these differences *variation*.

This means that … some tadpoles happen to have features that **help them survive** in this particular pond. The ones with longer tails can swim away faster from predators! They are more likely to survive until they become frogs and have tadpoles of their own.

Clue 3

Parents pass many of their features on to their offspring – for example, the length of their tails.

This means that … the tadpoles that survive long enough to become frogs and have tadpoles of their own, **will pass on their features** – including the ones that helped them survive.

What's the opposite of a spider?

Many things in nature have an opposite – something that is so **completely different** from them, that we can say it's like the reverse: hot and cold, light and dark, north and south, asleep and awake, alive and dead.

Can we use these **natural opposites** to answer this impossible question? A spider has eight legs, so perhaps its opposite is an animal with eight arms. A spider walks on land, so perhaps its opposite is an animal that swims in water. A spider has a tough outer skeleton, so perhaps its opposite is an animal with no skeleton at all.
Can you think of any creatures that might fit the bill?

Can you ask another 'impossible opposite' question? Use real opposites to come up with an answer!

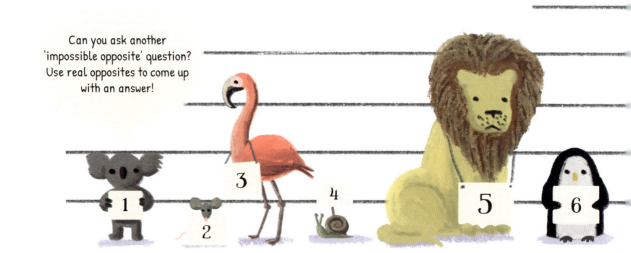

Why are animals such different sizes?

If you lined up the animals that live in any habitat – from a vast forest to a deep ocean – you'd find a **huge range of sizes**. The largest whales weigh around 2 trillion times more than the smallest water mites. Even more amazingly, the spread of sizes in each habitat is quite even, meaning you won't find one habitat where all the animals are HUGE, and another where they are all tiny. So why are the oceans home to creatures as large as blue whales, and as small as krill? And why do some mammals grow to the size of a truck, while others could perch on your little finger?

Each part of the world – even your garden – is packed with habitats of different sizes. A **whole forest** can be a habitat – but so can a **single leaf**, or the space under a **stone**. Being bigger may help an animal to stay warmer, move faster or catch larger prey, but bigger animals also use up energy and resources faster. If there are lots of big animals in one place, they all end up **competing** for the same types of food, drink and shelter – and they can't all win. Instead, nature seems to favour a wide range of animal sizes, with each species adapting to find food, water and shelter that other animals can't use. In nature, bigger doesn't mean better. **Different means better**! Elephants may be able to tear down entire trees, but they can't sip nectar from flowers like a hummingbird can. And lions might be great at catching zebra, but they'll never beat ants at creeping into a picnic and making off with the best snacks.

If everything is made of atoms, are feelings made of atoms?

Feelings happen in our brains and, like everything else in the universe, our brains are made of atoms. However, when we feel a feeling, our brains aren't simply firing up certain areas that mean 'fear' or 'joy' or 'excitement'. Like most impossible answers, it's not as simple as that! Scientists believe that every feeling has THREE parts.

1. Your brain notices changes in your body.
2. Your brain searches old memories and thoughts, trying to make sense of these changes.
3. Your brain produces a feeling that makes you want to behave in a certain way.

Imagine that you're standing at the top of a steep skate ramp. Before you've had a chance to think anything, your heart begins to beat faster. Your mouth feels dry. Your palms are sweaty. Your muscles tense up. **Signals from all these parts of your body reach your brain.** To work out what on earth is going on, your brain scans your memories for helpful clues. It uses this information to quickly produce a **feeling** that makes you want to behave in a certain way. If you have memories of successfully skating down a ramp, your brain might take note of your faster heart rate, dry mouth and sweaty palms, and produce a feeling of EXCITEMENT. But if you are standing at the top of that ramp for the first time (or you remember falling off in the past!) your brain might interpret those same body signals in a different way – producing a feeling of FEAR instead!

Feelings are reactions that happen in your brain, which is made from atoms but when your brain builds a feeling, it's drawing on your experiences and your imagination. So, we will never be able to take a bunch of atoms and use them to build a feeling. **Every feeling is unique to the person feeling it.**

Do plants have feelings?

Have you ever seen a happy houseplant, a terrified tree or a cross cactus? It's impossible to know for sure, because **we can't ask a plant how it's feeling**. But we can do some detective work, by designing experiments that give us clues. We know that human feelings happen in our brains, and that they help us respond to physical changes in our bodies. Plants don't have brains, but they **can** sense changes inside and around themselves, and respond to them.

Are they just feeling feelings in a different way?

To find out, one team of scientists grew a group of thale cress plants and played them a SCARY sound – the **crunching noise of caterpillars chewing leaves**. The plants responded as if they were really being attacked, flooding their leaves with chemicals that insects find disgusting. In another experiment, tomato plants being nibbled by insects released smelly chemicals into the air. When other tomatoes detected these **warning smells**, they began preparing for an attack themselves, by making their leaves toxic to insects. Were they feeling angry? And you know that lovely smell of freshly cut grass? That's an alarm signal too! Damaged leaves release smelly chemicals into the air. When grass on the other side of the lawn **detects** these chemicals, it begins moving nutrients away from the tips of its leaves into its roots. Are they doing this because they feel scared?

Probably not. Although plants CAN sense changes and respond to them, experiments like these have found **no evidence** that plants 'feel' angry or afraid before they react. Feelings help animals to react quickly, by comparing what is happening around them with past experiences. Plants don't seem to build these inner worlds. They just respond automatically. So you can climb that tree, roll on the grass, pick that apple or make a daisy chain without worrying – the plants (probably) don't mind at all!

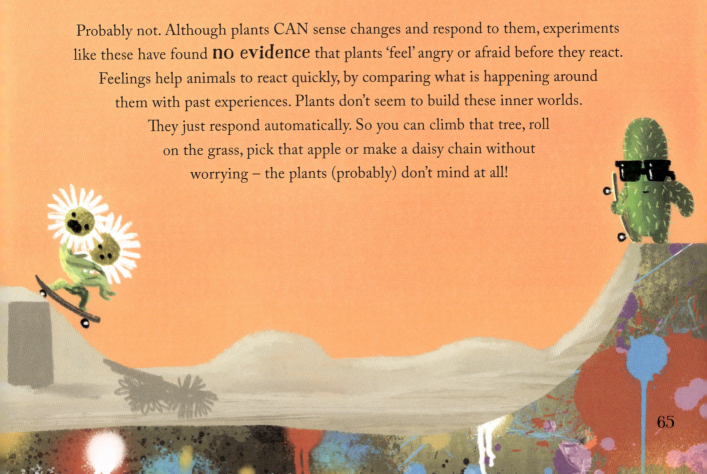

Where do new ideas come from?

Sometimes, you're strolling along or staring out of the window, when your brain lights up with a BRILLIANT idea! **Where do these brainwaves come from?** If you knew, perhaps you could pluck new ideas from your head when you REALLY need them – like on a rainy day at school, when your mind feels as blank as the page in front of you.

The bad news is, there IS NO MAP to help you find new ideas. The good news is, you don't need one! **New ideas aren't really that 'new' at all.** Your brain is just selecting some of the things you've already learned, seen, thought and experienced, and combining them in a new way. Even Isaac Newton (whose new ideas included gravity) pointed out that he was using the ideas and discoveries of the past. He described this as 'standing on the shoulders of giants'.

So where do we find some giants to stand on? Reading, learning, experimenting and playing are all ways to stuff your brain with raw material, which your imagination can connect in new ways. The second trick is **avoid trying too hard** to make these connections. Many people find that when they are TRYING to be creative, their minds go blank. Research has found that new ideas often come when we are doing something – or nothing – that lets our minds wander freely! With time and space, your brain might just decide to try out a new, unexpected pathway between two things that weren't previously connected. These **leaps of imagination** are the source of new ideas, and they're **impossible to predict**!

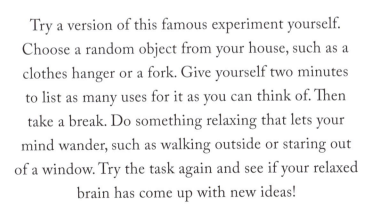

Try a version of this famous experiment yourself. Choose a random object from your house, such as a clothes hanger or a fork. Give yourself two minutes to list as many uses for it as you can think of. Then take a break. Do something relaxing that lets your mind wander, such as walking outside or staring out of a window. Try the task again and see if your relaxed brain has come up with new ideas!

Why are plants green?

This question is both possible and impossible to answer! Let's start with the possible part. We see plants (and everything else) because **light bounces off them** towards our eyes. Sunlight is a mixture of all the colours of the rainbow. All these colours hit a plant, but not all of them bounce off again. Some of them are **absorbed** (soaked up) by chemicals called pigments. Most plants contain a pigment called chlorophyll, which soaks up blue and red light, but reflects green. If only green light bounces off a plant towards our eyes, we see the leaf as green!

Now for the impossible part of the question – why do leaves bounce away green light in the first place? Leaves **use** the light they soak up to make food for the plant, so why not have black leaves that absorb EVERY colour? Some scientists think it's by accident – because the ancestor of all plants happened to be green. Other scientists think that it's not just an accident – and that bouncing away green light actually **helps plants**. Have you noticed how black surfaces get hotter than white ones on a sunny day? If a plant soaked up ALL the colours in sunlight, it might overheat, or become damaged (like our skin gets sunburned). We'll never know for sure. But imagine if you could avoid slapping on sunscreen ever again, just by becoming green! Would you?

How many trees are there in the whole world?

Trees are TREEmendous, TREErrific and exTREEmely important! They provide food and homes for **millions** of other living things. They clean up the air and anchor the soil in place. And their only waste products are water and the oxygen that we breathe! So, when we hear that humans are **chopping down trees** at an alarming rate, we want to know how many are left. We grab a clipboard and head to our nearest forest. And then … we realise there are so MANY trees that counting each one would take **far too long**.

But don't put your clipboard away yet. We can still **estimate** – or make a best guess. Imagine that you wanted to know how many blades of grass are in your back garden. It would take too long to count each one, but you could throw a hula hoop on the lawn and count every blade inside it. Then you could work out how many hula hoops it takes to cover the whole lawn, and multiply the numbers together to find your estimate. To estimate how many trees are growing on a whole PLANET, a team of scientists used their own version of the hula hoop – as big as two football fields – to sample trees in thousands of places around the world. Then they let computers crunch the data, and discovered that there are about **3.041 trillion trees on the planet** – around 400 for every person on Earth!

Once you've learned the estimation trick, you can use it to count ANYTHING – from the leaves on a tree to the hairs on your head (or the hairs on your dad's head if you're really pushed for time)! Pick your own impossible counting question, find your own version of the hula hoop, and start sampling!

1, 2, 3, 4, 5 ... 3.041 trillion

Why can't I just eat my favourite foods?

Wouldn't it be **amazing** if we could eat **chocolate, cheese or chips** all day long? If every breakfast was **pizza** and every snack an **ice cream sundae**? Unfortunately, for most people, eating ONLY their favourite foods would be a **recipe for disaster!** It all comes down to the reason we eat in the first place – to get hold of the ingredients essential for **building a body**! They include around **twenty-five different elements**, from carbon and calcium to tiny but important traces of iron and zinc. These elements **combine** in different ways to form millions of chemicals and structures, which work together to make you! Your body can assemble some of these chemicals itself, but others – known as nutrients – must be eaten ready-made.

In order for our bodies to **keep working** properly, we need to top up on nutrients constantly. Some are easy to get hold of – for example, a plate of chips is packed with carbohydrates (made from carbon, hydrogen and oxygen), plus sodium and chloride if you sprinkle on some salt. But we don't just need these five ingredients – we need all twenty-five! The **best way** to make sure you get hold of all the **elements** and **nutrients** you need is by eating a **rainbow of different foods**. This includes fruit, vegetables, lentils or beans, nuts and whole grains such as brown bread and brown rice.

How do soft foods make bones strong?

Have you ever heard the phrase 'You are what you eat'? It's a bit confusing, because we rarely **breakfast on bones**, or **toast teeth for lunch**! Most of our food is far softer. How on earth do **mushy vegetables** and **chewy cheese** help to build the **hard and tough** parts of our bodies? **Calcium** is part of the answer. A super-strong, metallic skeleton isn't just something you see in sci-fi movies – the metal calcium is one of the main **building blocks** of your bones and teeth, as well as your hair, skin and nails.

Dairy foods, beans, bony fish and leafy vegetables are good sources of calcium, but scientists have noticed that simply eating lots of calcium is **not enough** on its own. To **soak up** calcium and do the **construction work**, your body needs help from other nutrients, such as vitamin D and vitamin K. Luckily, these are often found in the same foods as calcium. Your skin also makes vitamin D when it's **bathed in sunlight** (although too much sunlight can be just as dangerous as too little). Food is such a big part of **staying healthy** that scientists are still working hard to investigate how ingredients from soft foods work together to build HARD bones. For now, you can rest assured that by **eating a rainbow** of different foods your body will **solve the mystery** itself.

How heavy is Earth?

It's impossible to pop an **entire planet** on to a pair of scales. But scientists CAN weigh a planet using **scientific laws**. These aren't the kind of laws that tell us how to behave. A scientific law is like a really good description of how things in the world DO behave. If we know certain things about the world, scientific laws help us to **predict** the rest. Just over 300 years ago, a scientist and all-round brainbox called Isaac Newton (page 24) wrote down one of the most famous scientific ideas of all – **the law of gravity**. It tells us that Earth's gravitational pull is what gives us **weight**. This means that if you were in outer space, with no gravity pulling on you, you would weigh nothing! This is the position Earth is in – so technically it's weightless!

However, don't put those scales away yet, because we **can** calculate Earth's mass. We often use the words 'mass' and 'weight' in the same way, but mass is actually a measure of how much 'stuff' something is made from. **This *doesn't* change as we move around the universe**. A typical ten-year-old would have a mass of about 32 kg whether they were standing on Earth, Mars or the Moon. With just three pieces of information – your mass, your weight and your distance from the centre of the planet – mathematicians can use the law of gravity to calculate Earth's mass too! It works out at around 6×10^{24} kg, which is a short way of writing **6,000,000,000,000,000,000,000,000 (6 quadrillion) kg**. So, it's probably a good thing you can't fit the planet on the bathroom scales!

Why is it easier to balance on a moving bike?

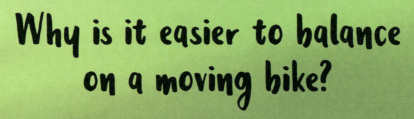

It's strange that we struggle to walk along a tightrope or a beam, but on wheels just 3 cm wide we can:

Zoooooooom down hills … *leap* through the air … and *lean* into corners … without tipping over!

It's far harder to **balance** on a bike that's **standing still**. But what are the **forces** (pushes or pulls) that stop bikes **tipping over** when they're moving? Bicycles were invented at least 200 years ago, but scientists still find this question impossible to answer once and for all!

For a long time, scientists thought it must be a force from the **spinning wheels** themselves. When a wheel or ball spins quickly, it becomes hard to tip or turn it to one side. An object like this is known as a **gyroscope**, and it's super stable. This helps to explain why a bike without a rider can **balance itself** if it's going fast enough. Find a flat, safe space, give your bike a push and see for yourself – the wheels just don't want to tip over! However, as soon as a person gets on the bike, the **extra weight** pushing down on the saddle and handlebars **cancels out** this gyroscope effect. So it can't be that.

Next, scientists looked at the **shape** of bikes themselves. The part that connects the handlebars and front wheel is tilted backwards, creating a gap called the trail. It helps to make a bike more stable. But one team of scientists built a bike without a trail, and it could **still balance** itself! Like the gyroscope effect, the trail can't be the only reason we find it easy to balance on a moving bike.

The way that your weight gets **spread out** when you're sitting on a bike is very important too. The centre of gravity is lower at the front of the bike than at the back. The front of a bike always tips to the side more quickly than the back. This causes the front wheel to automatically turn in the direction you are falling, instantly steering the bike back underneath you again! The **shape of a bike** is definitely important in helping it balance – it's why most bikes share a very similar design. However, it IS possible to fall off a bike (we've all done it), so something else must be going on too.

The missing part of the puzzle is YOU! As you pedal along enjoying the view, your brain is secretly hard at work. It detects every tiny wobble, and long before you even realise you're tipping over, it tells your muscles to make **tiny changes** that keep you upright, such as moving your body, pedalling harder on one side, or steering a fraction to one side. It takes a while for your brain to learn to do this on autopilot, which is why beginner cyclists are wobblier.

Although scientists still don't fully understand how bikes stay up, they know that each piece of the puzzle is equally important to stop you falling off.

Where do bruises come from and where do they go?

Ouch! We usually notice the **fall, scrape or bump** that causes a bruise to appear. The way in which they **disappear** is quieter and more **mysterious**. Bruises form when tiny blood vessels just underneath your skin get **damaged**, letting a little blood leak out. The blood gets **trapped**, making that area of skin look darker than the skin around it. The exact colour of a bruise depends on the colour of a person's skin, and on how old the bruise is. At first, bruises often look dark **brown, black, red or purple**. This is because blood is bright red, thanks to a colourful chemical called haemoglobin that carries oxygen around your body. Your body soon soaks the oxygen back up, and the trapped blood (and the bruise) becomes **bluish**. Next, your body starts to break up the haemoglobin bit by bit, to help build new red blood cells. At first it forms a greenish substance called biliverdin. If your bruise turns **green**, it's biliverdin you're seeing. Your body continues picking off and soaking up what it needs, breaking the biliverdin down even more to form bilirubin. This substance is light brown or yellow, so your bruise may look **brown or yellow** too. Finally, after around two weeks, the bruise disappears altogether. Your body has cleverly **reabsorbed and recycled** all the trapped blood. If only it could work out how to soak up embarrassment too!

Ouch!

Why can't I tickle myself?

Track down a member of your family and tell them you're going to tickle them in the name of science! **Watch what happens when you do**. Next, ask them to try tickling themselves. Do they wriggle, giggle and squirm in the same way? Most people find it IMPOSSIBLE to tickle themselves. To find out why, **scientists tickled people** while they were INSIDE a powerful brain scanner and watched the goings-on in their volunteers' brains.

They discovered that TWO parts of our brain get **activated** when we're being tickled – the part that uses information collected by our nerves to work out what's touching our skin, and the part that works out if we're feeling pleasure or pain. (With tickling, it's often hard to tell!) However, when we try to tickle ourselves, a THIRD part of our brain gets involved. This part **predicts** what it's going to feel like. Before the messages from your skin even reach your brain, the third part has reacted – by sending out signals that tell the normally tickle-sensitive parts of your brain to **ignore** what's about to happen! This ability to ignore things can be extremely helpful. It stops you collapsing into giggles every time you wash under your chin or put your hands on your hips!

Why do I like my friends more than I like other people?

Friends are groups of people who choose to spend lots of time speaking, playing, eating or just hanging out together. **But what makes us form these special relationships with some people but not others**? It's still impossible to explain, because scientists haven't been studying friendship for very long. However, from the studies they have done, one thing was easy to notice: **we tend to make friends with people who are like us**. For example, if you are ten years old and live in London, you probably have more friends who are ten years old and live in London than friends who are seven years old and live in Toronto. We pick friends who are like us in more surprising ways, too. Scientists have noticed that when we meet new people (potential friends!) we are more likely to feel connected to, or to 'click' with, people whose **expressions** and **body language** match our own. Good friends even **blink their eyes** a similar number of times every minute!

To find out more, scientists asked a group of volunteers to watch **funny, exciting** or **interesting** videos while sitting in a brain scanner, and watched to see how their brains **responded to different experiences**. Amazingly, volunteers with the most similar brain activity all turned out to be **good friends**! This suggests that friends' brains react to the world in similar ways. They are more likely to laugh at the same jokes, care about the same issues, and enjoy the same activities together. This is a big clue that you may like your friends more than other people, simply because **they remind you of YOU!**

Many mammals make friends – even vampire bats!

Do animals make friends?

For a long time, it seemed like most animals that hang around in groups prefer to spend time with (and help) members of their own family. But the more closely scientists look at animals that live in groups, the more examples of **animal friendships** they find – from birds and baboons, to hyenas and horses. Even sharks – who aren't known for their friendly personalities – seem to buddy up. When studying a group of more than 130 **blacktip reef sharks**, scientists noticed that certain sharks chose to **swim together**, while others tried to **avoid** each other. Their friendships (and feuds) lasted for years. **Dolphins** can also form **special relationships** with dolphins they aren't related to. Just like us, they seem to make friends with dolphins that are interested in the same things. For example, a few dolphins use animals called sponges as a tool to help them find food, and **they love to buddy up** to forage and feed.

Making friends may help animals to find **help** and **protection** when they need it, especially if they live in a bigger group. But animals **don't** seem to make friends for this reason alone. None of the animal friends that scientists have studied appear to keep a record in their memories of who owes who. Like us, animals probably make friends just **because it feels nice to have a friend**, without thinking about all the benefits it brings. For humans, these benefits include lower levels of stress, better health, a better immune system and even longer lives!

Goats have been spotted trying to make friends with humans! In one study, scientists set goats a task that was **impossible** for a goat to achieve – taking the lid off a box to get a reward. When the goats realized it was impossible, they tried to **make friends with nearby humans** by gazing at them … hoping that their new friends with hands would help!

Why don't we live forever?

People have been asking this question for thousands of years. It's true that **no animal lives forever.** Some animals have very short lives. Seahorses only live for **six years**, and mayflies die after just **one day** as an adult. (They have a lovely time though – they spend most of this day **dancing**!) Other animals have very long lives. Most elephants live for at least **70 years**, and some shellfish live for more than **500**! Humans also live for a long time. More than half of the babies born this year will live to celebrate more than **100 birthdays**.

Things like taking exercise, eating a rainbow of foods (see page 70), having good healthcare and getting lots of sleep can help humans to stay healthy and live long lives. But even if a person or animal never gets sick or injured, they will one day grow old and die. As we live our lives and have adventures, our bodies get **slowly worn down**. An older person's body also gets less good at repairing itself. By the time that starts to happen, they may have children, grandchildren, or nephews and nieces. To family members, they may pass on **inherited things** like their hair colour, face shape and even parts of their personality. To the world, they pass on the **special things** they have done, learned and created during their life. Together, we are all part of the **story of life** on Earth that has been going for billions of years. In this way, **a small part of everybody lives on forever.**

Why do trees live longer than animals?

Some animals live very long lives – Galapagos tortoises often celebrate their 100th birthday, and Greenland sharks can live for up to 500 years! But even these most ancient sharks are young compared to the **world's oldest trees**. Some bristlecone pines have been growing for more than **5,000 years**! When they were saplings, the Bronze Age was just getting started. So, what is the secret to their success?

Even when animals stop growing, their bodies are constantly **replacing** worn out or damaged cells. To do this, they rely on special cells called stem cells. But over time, the stem cells themselves get worn out. They become less good at **making copies** of themselves. Eventually, the animal can't replace damaged or worn out cells anymore, and it dies. Trees have a version of stem cells too. They're found in a part of the plant called the meristem. These cells **last longer** than animal stem cells and seem to be less affected by damage. Trees are different in other ways too. The meristem is the **only living part** of an ancient bristlecone pine that is thousands of years old. New bark, leaves and cones **grow every year**, and the ancient wood of the trunk and roots is not properly alive at all. Trees are also better at **recovering from damage**. If a plant loses a branch in a storm, or its leaves get eaten by insects, it can replace them. Very few animals can regrow missing parts.

Sadly, it's impossible to copy the anti-ageing tricks of trees to make animals live for longer. There are just too many differences between us. But we can **celebrate** all the things that animals can do that plants can't – such as **exploring** different places, **eating** delicious food and **snuggling up** to read brilliant books at bedtime.

I am only 100 years old!

Why am I yawning?

Your mouth starts to open … you take a long, deep breath … your head tilts back … your eyes water and close a little … your mouth stretches as WIDE as it can … and you breathe out, with a sleepy sigh.

Everyone knows what it's like to yawn. We begin doing it **several months** before we are born! Most animals with backbones have been spotted yawning too, from fish and frogs, to birds and big cats. The big difference is that no one ever tells a **yawning tiger** that they must be tired, and it's time for bed. (**No one would dare**!) But does yawning really mean a person or animal is **tired**? Scientists aren't so sure. Although millions of yawns happen every second of every day, scientists ignored them for a long time! We've only just started to investigate yawning properly. Here are the things we do know about yawning:

It's contagious! Have you yawned yet, while reading this page? Watching, reading or even thinking about yawning can bring one on.

It's impossible to yawn just because you want to. And when other people are watching too closely, you might be put off from yawning at all!

It's impossible to stop once you've started – even if you know the next words you hear will be, 'Bedtime'! Even pinching your nose won't stop a yawn, and if you try and keep your mouth closed, you'll feel strange – like the yawn is stuck in your body, waiting to come out!

Yawning often happens close to sleep … but it doesn't always mean we're tired. For many animals, most yawning actually happens soon after **waking up**, *after* a sleep. We yawn more when we're watching something or studying than when we're doing something hands-on. So, yawning may be our body's way of giving our brain and body a **quick boost**. Some scientists have suggested that yawning could help **cool our brain down** when it's getting a bit too warm. Or perhaps it's about **communication** – which would explain why it's so easy to 'catch' a yawn. Matching what other people are doing can help humans to make friends (find out how on page 78), so yawning may be an ancient way for animals to show that they understand how others are feeling – a skill called **empathy**. It's still impossible to explain exactly why we yawn, but trying to find out could help us to understand all sorts of other things too. **Far from being yawn-some**, yawning is one of the most **exciting** areas of science around!

Why can't I remember falling asleep?

You've done it **thousands of times**, but you still have no idea what it feels like! Don't worry – no one remembers the moment they fall asleep each night. It's because of the way that our brains make memories. Part of your brain called the hippocampus helps to change **short-term memories** (like what happened at the start of this page) into long-term memories (like what happened on your last birthday). After this change has happened, the short-term memory fades to make room for more. If you wake a few seconds after falling asleep, you will **still remember** the thoughts you were thinking or the sounds you heard as you fell asleep. These are still active in your short-term memory, and it won't feel like you've been sleeping at all. But if you fall asleep for longer than a few minutes, these short-term memories **fade away**. They NEVER get transferred to your long-term memory because your hippocampus is **asleep too**! Even if you wake up just six minutes after falling asleep, everything you were thinking or feeling at that moment will have faded away. This is also why you should keep a notepad by your bed and write all those BRILLIANT world-changing ideas that come to you as your head hits the pillow … if you leave it until the morning, they'll be lost **forever**!

A typical human yawn lasts six seconds.

83

How do animals know where they are going when they are underground?

Living underground is a great way to protect yourself from weather and predators. From rabbits and gerbils to chipmunks and woodchucks, more than 250 types of rodents dig burrows for sleeping or nesting, connected by subterranean tunnels. They are **excellent engineers**, but even they haven't figured out how to install lights or signs! Some rodents, called mole rats, can **barely see at all**, yet they somehow dig and then find their way around huge underground neighbourhoods in the **darkest dark**. They can't afford to leave route-finding up to luck, because digging uses up to **3,400 times more energy** than moving about on the surface. So how do mole rats and other rodents make sure they're moving in the right direction? Could they be following sounds or smells? Or just remembering where they dug in the past?

It's unlikely. These methods work best over short distances, and the burrows of some mole rats are like **mazes**, twisting and turning through the soil for hundreds or even thousands of metres. A big clue comes from the **long, straight tunnels** dug by silvery mole rats, which always run from north to south. This suggests that mole rats can sense **Earth's magnetic field** and use it to help them find their way! The next step towards answering this question will be to find out **which part** of a rodent's body acts as their built-in satnav.

Other animals seem able to sense Earth's magnetic field too, including birds, fish, butterflies and termites.

Why do I dream?

Your brain might seem to switch off when you go to sleep, but it's actually **hard at work** doing jobs that it can't do when you're awake! During the night, it cycles in and out of different stages of sleep, from **light dozing** to **deep slumber**. During one stage of sleep called Rapid Eye Movement (REM) sleep, our brains can be **even more active** than when we're awake! You can tell if someone is in REM sleep because their eyes flicker behind their closed eyelids, and they breathe more quickly. If someone wakes up during REM sleep, they can often remember the thoughts, pictures and even feelings that were dancing through their sleeping mind. However, if they are woken up from other stages of sleep, this is far less likely. This tells us that most dreams (and nightmares) seem to happen during REM sleep. Luckily, our brain **relaxes** the rest of our muscles so much during REM sleep that we can't **act out our dreams**!

Most people spend up to a quarter of their night's sleep in REM sleep – adding up to six YEARS of dreaming over an average lifetime! We know what dreams are. We know when they happen. **But we don't yet know why our brains spend six years making up stories.** Perhaps it's a side effect of all the jobs your brain is busy doing while you're asleep. Or perhaps your brain is purposely replaying new things that you've learned, as a way of practising or remembering them.

How do I know I'm not dreaming right now?

You could ask someone to **tickle you** to see if you wake up! But seriously, this is a question that scientists have tried to answer too. Our brains use the information collected by our senses to 'build' a picture of the world inside our heads. Brains are so good at **world building**, that they keep on doing it even when we sleep. This is why it's possible for you to dream about people and places you've never seen before, and experiences you've never had – like having conversations with a pet! Hundreds of years ago, a **philosopher** (someone who loves to ponder impossible questions) began to wonder – if dreams can seem real, how do we know that the 'real' world isn't just another dream? Are we actually dreaming *all the time*? Since then, all kinds of different people have tried to figure out the answer to this question. One answer comes from a group of scientists who have nothing to do with brain OR sleep science! **Physicists** are scientists who study what the universe is made of. Over the last 100 years, they have discovered that the universe is built from **particles** and **rays** that we simply can't detect with our human senses. These **hidden details** of the universe are incredibly complicated, but also incredibly consistent. Physicists all around the world get the same results whenever they measure them. This is a clue that reality is **far too strange** and complex for our brains to conjure up … even in our wildest dreams!

How do we know what dinosaurs were like?

The last dinosaurs died nearly **66 million years ago**, long before humans were around to meet, draw or photograph them. Yet we see dinosaurs everywhere – starring in **movies**, drawing crowds to **museums**, roaring at us from **T-shirts** and terrorising the **toy cupboard**. Many people find it easier to describe a *Tyrannosaurus rex* than a tapir, even though tapirs are still alive! How do palaeontologists (scientists who study dinosaurs) know so much about creatures that are **so long extinct**?

As with other types of science, studying dinosaurs is all about **piecing together clues**. The best clues come in the form of **fossils** – very special rocks that show us who lived on the planet long ago. Fossils aren't the actual bones, teeth or claws of a dinosaur, but they show us the shape of these body parts. If palaeontologists find enough fossilised bones from a dinosaur, they can fit them together like a **3D jigsaw** to work out what the animal's entire skeleton looked like. Softer parts like muscles, skin and feathers don't usually form fossils, so palaeontologists use some extra clues to make a best guess. They compare fossils to today's animals. By doing this, they can even make a best guess about a dinosaur's colours, sounds and behaviour. However, even the most **careful scientists** sometimes get it REALLY WRONG!

When the first *Stegosaurus* fossil was discovered, scientists thought its bony plates must have covered its back like tiles! It took ten years to work out that the plates stood straight up.

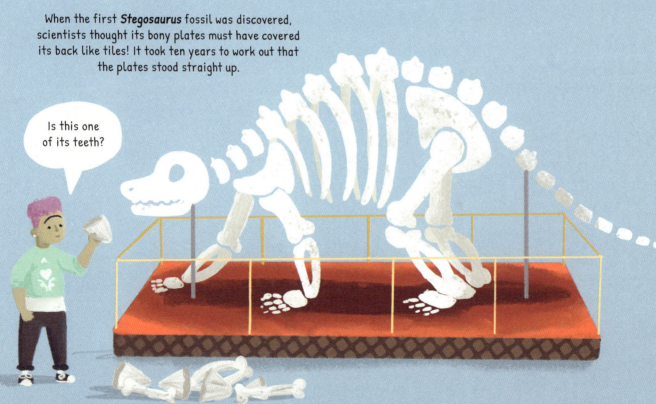

Is this one of its teeth?

Working out how dinosaurs behaved is even harder. **Pachycephalosaurus** skeletons have a bony dome on their heads that looks like a cycle helmet. At first scientists assumed these were used for head-butting competitions. But as they learned more about this dinosaur's skeleton, they realised its neck would have been far too weak. The domes were probably just for showing off, like the tail of a peacock.

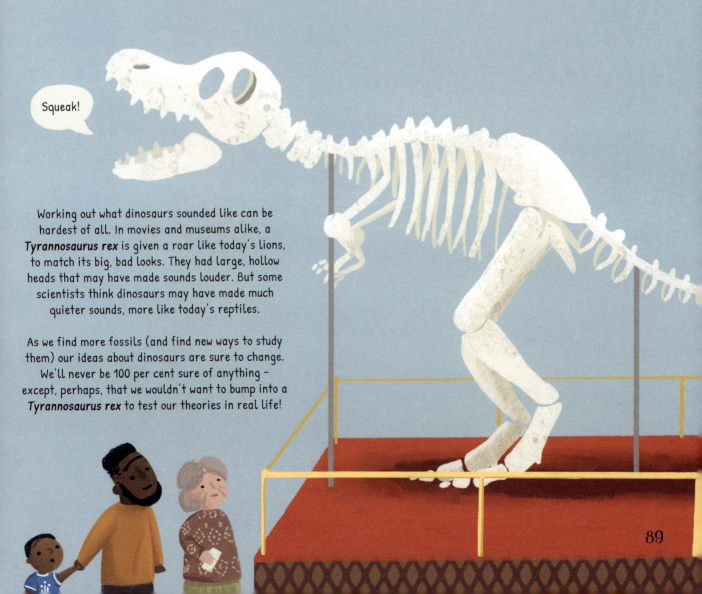

Working out what dinosaurs sounded like can be hardest of all. In movies and museums alike, a **Tyrannosaurus rex** is given a roar like today's lions, to match its big, bad looks. They had large, hollow heads that may have made sounds louder. But some scientists think dinosaurs may have made much quieter sounds, more like today's reptiles.

As we find more fossils (and find new ways to study them) our ideas about dinosaurs are sure to change. We'll never be 100 per cent sure of anything – except, perhaps, that we wouldn't want to bump into a **Tyrannosaurus rex** to test our theories in real life!

How do we know what stars are made of?

Twinkle, twinkle, little star, how I wonder what you are ...

When this famous song was written in 1806, most people had no idea what the twinkling **pinpricks of light** in the night sky were made of. After 200 years of wondering, at last we do have some answers. No one has visited a star to check, but we don't have to. **Light from stars travels to us**! Scientists began by looking more closely at light from our nearest star – the **Sun**. Sunlight appears to be colourless, or white, but is actually a mixture of many different colours of light. You can see them by holding up a glass of water in a ray of sunlight, in front of a black or white wall. As the sunlight travels through the water, the colours are **split up**, so each one hits the wall in a slightly different place creating a **rainbow effect**.

The Sun and other stars glow because they are HOT. Hot things on Earth glow too, from fires to lightbulbs. Amazingly, every chemical on Earth – including all the different elements – releases and soaks up a very specific mixture of coloured light. **Discovering this gave scientists a way to find out what the Sun is made of**! All they had to do was split sunlight into a rainbow of colours. The colours that they saw (and those that were missing) told them which types of glowing atoms were at the Sun's surface. It's a bit like a barcode for a star! They showed that the Sun contains hydrogen, sodium and calcium – at least on its surface, which is the part that gives out the light.

It took longer to find out what else was **inside** the Sun, and other stars. To test this, scientists first had to be able to detect other types of particles and rays. Today, we know that **all stars** contain lots of hydrogen (their fuel) and quite a lot of helium (which is made from the hydrogen, deep inside the star). Analysing light and other types of radiation from stars has helped us work out that **stars are the factories of the universe** – the places where most elements we find on Earth are made. This includes the elements that build your body – meaning that **you are made of stardust**!

If we are made of stardust, how did it get to Earth?

Most of the building blocks of our bodies were formed in stars. Not the stars you can see in the night sky, but in stars that **burned out** billions of years ago. When a star uses up most of its hydrogen fuel, it begins to **change**. The atoms that formed in its firey insides may be slowly **swept out** into space. Or the star might **EXPLODE** and scatter its stardust across the galaxy. Many elements are ONLY formed as a star burns out. The universe is full of **drifting stardust**. It's the raw material for new stars, planets, moons, comets and asteroids. Our own Sun and solar system were formed around **4.6 billion years ago**, from the dust left behind by old stars. The elements in the dust gradually came together in different ways to make our planet, and the things on it. At first these were simple chemicals and minerals such as water, and rocks. Then more complicated chemicals began to form, and finally living things – including us.

Some of the stardust that **builds your body** may be as ancient as the universe or the solar system itself! Some landed on Earth more recently, in **comets**, **asteroids** and smaller **meteorites**. Much of the stardust that formed Earth seems to have been made by medium-sized stars that expand and then shrink as they run out of fuel, instead of exploding. Elements formed inside this type of star include molybdenum – one of the important **ingredients** in our bodies. Around **40,000 tonnes** of stardust rain down on Earth every year, but most of it is far too small to see. On Earth, scientists have even found grains of stardust 3 billion years older than our own Sun that crashed to Earth inside a massive meteorite. It's impossible to say exactly when and where the building blocks of your body were made, but you can be sure that **every atom** has been on an **epic adventure** through space and time to get to **you**, reading this book, right now.

The adventures continue ...

These IMPOSSIBLE QUESTIONS have taken you through space and time, up distant mountains, deep beneath oceans, on a tour of the human brain and even (fearlessly) into the **very depths of your nose**. As you travelled, did you notice that every answer had something in common?

(It's every scientist's favourite answer ...)

We don't know (yet)!

Most WORLD CHANGING discoveries and ideas began with an IMPOSSIBLE QUESTION.

Scientists have looked for answers in different ways. Some peer through **telescopes** or down **microscopes**. Some use carefully planned **experiments** with fancy machines and labs. Others experiment in their minds, using **mathematics**. Some talk to people (or listen to guinea pigs). And some stumble across an answer quite by accident. **There are so many different ways to do science.**

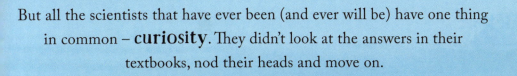

But all the scientists that have ever been (and ever will be) have one thing in common – **curiosity**. They didn't look at the answers in their textbooks, nod their heads and move on.

They asked more questions.

There's only one group of people that are EVEN BETTER at asking questions than scientists are …

CHILDREN

just like you!

It's easy. Next time you notice something strange (in the real world, or in your thoughts) don't just pass on by. Stop, look more closely, and let your curiosity show you which way to go.

Ask an **IMPOSSIBLE QUESTION**.